Written by Richard Bodley Scott, assisted by
Nik Gaukroger, James Hamilton,
Paul Robinson, Xavier Codina & David Cáceres

First published in Great Britain in 2009 by Osprey Publishing Ltd.

Osprey Publishing, Midland House, West Way, Botley, Oxford OX2 0PH, UK
443 Park Avenue South, New York, NY 10016, USA
E-mail: info@ospreypublishing.com

Slitherine Software UK Ltd., The White Cottage, 8 West Hill Avenue, Epsom, KT 19 8LE, UK
E-mail: info@slitherine.co.uk

A CIP catalogue record for this book is available from the British Library

ISBN: 978 1 84603 479 4

Rules system written by Richard Bodley Scott, Simon Hall, and Terry Shaw
Page layout and cover concept by Myriam Bell
Index by Michael Parkin
Typeset in Joanna Pro and Sleepy Hollow
Cover artwork by Peter Dennis
Photography by Duncan MacFarlane – Wargames Illustrated, Eric Bonsall, Nick Bennett, Will & Rickard
Page design features supplied by istockphoto.com
All artwork and cartography © Osprey Publishing Ltd
Originated by PDQ Media, UK
Printed in China through Worldprint Ltd

09 10 11 12 13 10 9 8 7 6 5 4 3 2 1

FOR A CATALOGUE OF ALL BOOKS PUBLISHED BY OSPREY MILITARY AND AVIATION PLEASE CONTACT:

NORTH AMERICA
Osprey Direct, c/o Random House Distribution Center, 400 Hahn Road, Westminster, MD 21157
E-mail: uscustomerservice@ospreypublishing.com

ALL OTHER REGIONS
Osprey Direct, The Book Service Ltd, Distribution Centre, Colchester Road, Frating Green, Colchester, Essex, CO7 7DW
E-mail: customerservice@ospreypublishing.com

FOR DETAILS OF ALL GAMES PUBLISHED BY SLITHERINE SOFTWARE UK LTD
E-mail: info@slitherine.co.uk

Osprey Publishing is supporting the Woodland Trust, the UK's leading woodland conservation charity, by funding the dedication of trees.

www.ospreypublishing.com
www.slitherine.com

CONTENTS

INTRODUCTION

This book covers the Early Medieval period in western and northern Europe, commonly known as the "Dark Ages", from 496 AD until 1070 AD.

Following the collapse of the Western Roman Empire at the end of the 5th century, the post-Roman world was divided into a number of kingdoms, each ruled by the "barbarian" grouping that had come to control it during the last days of the Empire. After the initial round of wars, the Franks held most of modern France and also controlled a substantial area of Germany, the Visigoths held Spain, the Ostrogoths held Italy and the Vandals held North Africa.

Continuity with the Roman Empire, however, was at first considerable. Many of the "barbarian" armies, though of Germanic tribal origin, were in fact originally Late Roman field armies, and continued to use Late Roman methods of supporting the soldiers. Each soldier was assigned to share a portion of the land of a Roman landowner, from which he drew his pay.

Post-Roman British Commander

In the mid 6th century the Eastern Roman (Byzantine) Empire launched a counter-offensive, reconquering Africa from the Vandals, Italy from the Ostrogoths and part of southern Spain from the Visigoths. Soon after, however, they lost the north of Italy to the invading Lombards.

In the surviving "barbarian" kingdoms Roman institutions started to lose their attraction. "Roman" land-holders acquired ethnic status as "Franks" or "Goths", whereas the poorest "Romans" lost their free status entirely and became serfs. During the course of the 6th century soldiers came to acquire land in their own right, so that by the beginning of the 7th century the military class corresponded to the free land-owning class – although at this stage military service was not specifically tied to land tenure. During the 7th century military service became more selective, and local nobles gained the right to raise troops – theoretically on behalf of the crown.

In the early 8th century Muslim armies invaded Spain and conquered the Visigothic Kingdom, leaving only small areas in the mountainous north independent and Christian. At about the same time, the fragmented Merovingian Frankish Kingdom was being reunited by the Mayors of the Palace, who eventually ascended the throne as the Carolingian dynasty. Under Charlemagne, the Frankish Empire came to include modern France, Germany and northern Italy, the largest single

political entity in the West since the fall of the Western Roman Empire.

Partly as a consequence of its success, and the resulting lack of new regions to pillage and conquer, military service became less attractive, so that it became necessary to pass laws compelling military service, based on the amount of land held.

In the 9th century, as well as suffering from endemic internal strife, the Frankish Empire came under attack from Vikings in the West and Magyars in the East. At the end of the century it split permanently into separate kingdoms corresponding to modern France and Germany. As the regional nobility increased in power, the power of the kings declined, so that when the Capetian dynasty acquired the throne of West Francia (France) at the end of the 10th century, the king controlled only a small part of the territory of the kingdom.

Viking Huscarl

Anglo-Saxon England also came under Viking attack, much of northern and eastern England coming under Danish control in the later 9th century, and the whole Kingdom of England being ruled by Danish kings for 30 years in the early 11th century. The Normans, who conquered England in 1066, were also of Viking descent.

TROOP NOTES

There appears to have been a significant alteration in Western European infantry tactics around the end of the 6th century. Prior to that date Frankish weapon burials include heavy throwing spears (*angones*) similar to Roman *pila*, throwing axes (*franciscae*) and single-handed battle axes. In 7th century burials these disappear, while spearheads become more substantial. Shields also became larger. Similar changes are seen in Anglo-Saxon England at around the same time. It seems likely that these changes represent a transition from a more individualistic fighting style to shield-wall tactics.

The date we have chosen for the transition from lancer cavalry to medieval knights is entirely arbitrary, as this was probably a gradual and subtle change. By the mid 11th century, however, Western European cavalry had certainly acquired a huge ascendancy over their eastern counterparts in close combat.

ACKNOWLEDGEMENT

In drawing up this book we have been heavily influenced by Guy Halsall's *Warfare and Society in the Barbarian West* 450-900.

POST-ROMAN BRITISH

This list covers Post-Roman British armies (except in Wales) from the late 4th century AD, when local warlords were probably left to fend for themselves in the north and west, until the collapse of the lowland kingdoms at the end of the 6th century. Thereafter it continues to cover the northern British kingdoms of Elmet (annexed by Northumbria in 616 or 626), Gododdin (annexed by Bernicia c.638), Rheged (annexed by Northumbria some time before 730), and Strathclyde (annexed by the Scots between 1019 and 1053). Also, the south-western kingdoms of Dumnonia and Cornwall (finally annexed by England by the reign of Edward the Confessor 1042–1066).

TROOP NOTES

Drilled troops represent remnants of the Roman garrisons. We assume that these survived the withdrawal of Roman authority for a number of years and initially formed the basis of local warlord forces before finally fading away.

The choice of classification for the undrilled spearmen is to allow for various interpretations of the limited evidence. Our feeling is that the spearmen of the lowland kingdoms would be more likely to qualify as heavy foot, while those of the hillier regions, such as Rheged, might be more appropriately classified as medium foot.

"Arthur's companions" are to allow for the very faint possibility that the later legends of King Arthur's Knights of the Round Table preserve some folk memory of this era. If so a survival or revival of the *Equites Catafractarii*, part of the *Dux Britanniarum*'s command as listed in the Late Roman *Notitia Dignitatum*, might conceivably have provided the model. We incorporate this wild speculation for the benefit of those so inclined. Even so, it is extremely unlikely that they would still have had full cataphract equipment.

Roman allies represent a possible return of the field army c.416.

British Spearmen

POST-ROMAN BRITISH STARTER ARMY		
Commander-in-Chief	1	Inspired Commander (Arthur)
Sub-commanders	2	2 x Troop Commander
Arthur's companions	1 BG	4 bases of cavalry: Superior, Armoured, Drilled Cavalry – Lancers, Swordsmen
Cavalry	2 BGs	Each comprising 4 bases of cavalry: Superior, Protected, Undrilled Cavalry – Light Spear, Swordsmen
Light cavalry	1 BG	4 bases of light cavalry: Average, Unprotected, Undrilled, Light Horse – Javelins, Light Spear
Spearmen	4 BGs	Each comprising 8 bases of spearmen: Average, Protected, Undrilled Heavy Foot – Light Spear, Swordsmen
Archers	2 BGs	Each comprising 6 bases of archers: Average, Unprotected, Undrilled Light Foot – Bow
Camp	1	Unfortified camp
Total	10 BGs	Camp, 16 mounted bases, 44 foot bases, 3 commanders

BUILDING A CUSTOMISED LIST USING OUR ARMY POINTS

Choose an army based on the maxima and minima in the list below. The following special instructions apply to this army:

- Commanders should be depicted as cavalry.
- British allied commanders' contingents must conform to the Post-Roman British allies list below, but the troops in the contingent are deducted from the minima and maxima in the main list.
- Before 425 armies must contain at least 4 bases of drilled cavalry and 24 bases of drilled infantry. This is to represent the remnant Roman forces that would be the initial troop base.
- Except that those in a British allied contingent can be classified differently from those in the main army, all undrilled foot spearmen must be classified the same. i.e. all Medium Foot Light Spear, Swordsmen, or all Heavy Foot Light Spear, Swordsmen, or all Heavy Foot Defensive Spearmen.
- Welsh allies cannot be used with Saxon *foederati*/ mercenaries.

British Cavalry

POST-ROMAN BRITISH

Territory Types: Agricultural, Hilly, Woodlands											
C-in-C		Inspired Commander/Field Commander/Troop Commander						80/50/35	1		
Sub-commanders		Field Commander/Troop Commander						50/35	0-2		
British allied commanders		Field Commander/Troop Commander						40/25	0-3		
Troop name		Troop Type				Capabilities		Points per base	Bases per BG	Total bases	
		Type	Armour	Quality	Training	Shooting	Close Combat				
Core Troops											
Cavalry	Only before 500	Cavalry	Armoured	Average	Drilled	-	Light Spear, Swordsmen	13	4-6	0-6	4-18
	Any date	Cavalry	Armoured	Superior	Undrilled	-	Light Spear, Swordsmen	16	4-6		
		Cavalry	Protected	Superior Average	Undrilled	-	Light Spear, Swordsmen	12 9	4-6	0-16	
"Arthur's companions"	Only before 540	Cavalry	Armoured	Superior	Drilled Undrilled	-	Lancers, Swordsmen	17 16	4	0-4	
Spearmen	Only before 500	Medium or Heavy Foot	Protected	Average Poor	Drilled	-	Light Spear, Swordsmen	7 5	6-8	24-144	
	Any date	Medium or Heavy Foot	Protected	Average Poor	Undrilled	-	Light Spear, Swordsmen	6 4	6-8		
	Only from 600	Heavy Foot	Protected	Average Poor	Undrilled	-	Defensive Spearmen	6 4	6-8		
Optional Troops											
Light cavalry		Light Horse	Unprotected	Average	Undrilled	Javelins	Light Spear	7	4	0-4	
Archers		Light Foot	Unprotected	Average	Undrilled	Bow	-	5	6-8	0-12	
Saxon foederati or mercenaries	Only before 442	Heavy Foot	Protected	Average	Undrilled	-	Impact Foot, Swordsmen	7	6-8	0-12	
Allies											
Roman allies (Only before 425) – Dominate Roman – See Field of Glory Companion 5: *Legions Triumphant: Imperial Rome at War*											
Saxon allies (Only before 442) – Early Anglo-Saxon, Bavarian, Frisian, Old Saxon or Thuringian – See Field of Glory Companion 5: *Legions Triumphant: Imperial Rome at War*											
Viking allies (Only from 790)											
Welsh allies (Only before 580) – Early Welsh											

POST-ROMAN BRITISH ALLIES

Allied commander		Field Commander/Troop Commander						40/25	1	
Troop name		Troop Type				Capabilities		Points per base	Bases per BG	Total bases
		Type	Armour	Quality	Training	Shooting	Close Combat			
Cavalry	Only before 500	Cavalry	Armoured	Average	Drilled	-	Light Spear, Swordsmen	13	4	0-6
	Any date	Cavalry	Armoured	Superior	Undrilled	-	Light Spear, Swordsmen	16	4	
		Cavalry	Protected	Superior Average	Undrilled	-	Light Spear, Swordsmen	12 9	4-6	
Spearmen	Only before 500	Medium or Heavy Foot	Protected	Average Poor	Drilled	-	Light Spear, Swordsmen	7 5	6-8	6-32
	Any date	Medium or Heavy Foot	Protected	Average Poor	Undrilled	-	Light Spear, Swordsmen	6 4	6-8	
	Only from 600	Heavy Foot	Protected	Average Poor	Undrilled	-	Defensive Spearmen	6 4	6-8	
Archers		Light Foot	Unprotected	Average	Undrilled	Bow	-	5	4	0-4

EARLY WELSH

Following the contraction of Roman control of Britain in the late 4th century AD, the various Christian British states in Wales were left to govern themselves. The country was divided into a number of separate kingdoms, the largest being Gwynedd in the north west and Powys in the east. As the British kingdoms of southern and eastern Britain fell to the Anglo-Saxons, pressure came to be felt by the Welsh. At the Battle of Chester (613 or 616), the forces of Powys and other British kingdoms were defeated by the Northumbrians under Æthelfrith. After this battle land contact was severed between Wales and the northern British kingdoms of Elmet, Gododdin, Rheged and Strathclyde.

In 633, Cadwallon ap Cadfan of Gwynedd, in alliance with Penda of Mercia, defeated Edwin of Northumbria and controlled Northumbria for a period before being defeated and killed by Oswald of Bernicia. Thereafter Gwynedd, like the other Welsh kingdoms, was on the defensive against the rising power of Mercia. Powys originally extended well into areas now part of England, but gradually lost these territories to Mercia. Offa's Dyke, built by the Mercians in the 8th century, formed the new border.

Owing to the Welsh system of inheritance, which divided a father's holding amongst all his sons, it was rare for any single leader to control the whole of the country, and internecine strife was common. Rhodri Mawr (Rhodri the Great), King of Gwynedd in the second half of the 9th century, managed to extend his rule over Powys and Ceredigion, and defeated a Danish incursion in 856. After his death the kingdoms were divided again between his sons. Viking raids became commonplace, especially in the later 10th century.

Welsh Spearman

The next ruler to unite most of Wales was Gruffydd ap Llywelyn, also originally King of Gwynedd, in the later 11th century. In 1055, in alliance with Ælfgar of Mercia, he defeated the English army under Ralph the Timid at Hereford. He won another victory the following year. In 1063, however, he was defeated by the English under Harold Godwinson and subsequently murdered by his own men.

At the time of the Norman conquest of England in 1066, the most powerful ruler in Wales was Bleddyn ap Cynfyn, king of Gwynedd and Powys. Soon afterwards, the Normans began to make incursions into Wales, overrunning Gwent in the south east by 1070, and reaching Deheubarth in the south west by 1074. Following the death of Bleddyn ap Cynfyn in 1075, civil war broke out in Wales, allowing the Normans to make inroads into North Wales. Much of Gwynedd was seized in 1081 following the treacherous capture of Gruffydd ap Cynan at a parley. Morgannwg, in the south, was annexed in 1090, Deheubarth in 1093. Welsh fortunes were at a low ebb.

In 1094, however, the Welsh revolted and some of the lost territories were restored to Welsh rule.

A strong kingdom of Gwynedd was rebuilt by Gruffydd ap Cynan. The Normans were heavily defeated at Crug Mawr in 1136 and Ceredigion recovered. Powys also remained independent.

This list covers Welsh armies from the late 4th century until 1100.

EARLY WELSH STARTER ARMY		
Commander-in-Chief	1	Field Commander
Sub-commanders	2	2 x Troop Commander
Cavalry	1 BG	4 bases of cavalry: Superior, Armoured, Undrilled Cavalry – Light Spear, Swordsmen
Cavalry	2 BGs	Each comprising 4 bases of cavalry: Superior, Protected, Undrilled Cavalry – Light Spear, Swordsmen
Spearmen	3 BGs	Each comprising 10 bases of spearmen: Average, Protected, Undrilled Medium Foot – Light Spear, Swordsmen
Attecotti warriors	2 BGs	Each comprising 6 bases of Attecotti warriors: Superior, Protected, Undrilled, Medium Foot – Impact Foot, Swordsmen
Javelin skirmishers	1 BG	8 bases of javelin skirmishers: Average, Unprotected, Undrilled Light Foot – Javelins, Light Spear
Camp	1	Unfortified camp
Total	9 BGs	Camp, 12 mounted bases, 50 foot bases, 3 commanders

BUILDING A CUSTOMISED LIST USING OUR ARMY POINTS

Choose an army based on the maxima and minima in the list below. The following special instructions apply to this army:

- Commanders should be depicted as cavalry or spearmen.
- Cavalry can always dismount as Heavy Foot, Armoured or Protected (as mounted type), Superior, Impact Foot, Swordsmen.
- Welsh allied commanders' contingents must conform to the Early Welsh allies list below, but the troops in the contingent are deducted from the minima and maxima in the main list.
- Irish and Viking (Ostmen) allies can be used together, but not with Saxons.
- Saxon allies cannot be used with Votadini or Attecotti.

Welsh Commander

EARLY WELSH

EARLY WELSH										
Territory Types: Hilly, Mountains. (Only before 650): Agricultural.										
C-in-C	Inspired Commander/Field Commander/Troop Commander						80/50/35	1		
Sub-commanders	Field Commander						50	0-2		
	Troop Commander						35	0-3		
Welsh allied commanders	Field Commander/Troop Commander						40/25	0-2		
Troop name	Troop Type				Capabilities		Points per base	Bases per BG	Total bases	
	Type	Armour	Quality	Training	Shooting	Close Combat				
Core Troops										
Cavalry	Cavalry	Armoured	Superior	Undrilled	-	Light Spear, Swordsmen	16	4	0-4	4-12
	Cavalry	Protected	Superior	Undrilled	-	Light Spear, Swordsmen	12	4-6	0-12	
Spearmen	Medium Foot	Protected	Average	Undrilled	-	Light Spear, Swordsmen	6	6-10	24-154	
		Unprotected					5			
Javelin skirmishers	Light Foot	Unprotected	Average	Undrilled	Javelins	Light Spear	4	6-8	6-18	
Optional Troops										
Votadini warriors (Only before 540)	Medium Foot	Protected	Average	Undrilled	-	Impact Foot, Swordsmen	7	8-12	0-12	
Attecotti warriors (Only before 540)	Medium Foot	Protected	Superior	Undrilled	-	Impact Foot, Swordsmen	9	6-8		
Allies										
Irish mercenary allies (Only from 1075) – Norse Irish										
Saxon allies – Middle Anglo-Saxon or Anglo-Danish										
Viking allies (Only from 790)										

EARLY WELSH ALLIES

EARLY WELSH ALLIES									
Allied commander	Field Commander/Troop Commander						40/25	0-2	
Troop name	Troop Type				Capabilities		Points per base	Bases per BG	Total bases
	Type	Armour	Quality	Training	Shooting	Close Combat			
Cavalry	Cavalry	Armoured	Superior	Undrilled	-	Light Spear, Swordsmen	16	4	0-4
	Cavalry	Protected	Superior	Undrilled	-	Light Spear, Swordsmen	12	4	
Spearmen	Medium Foot	Protected	Average	Undrilled	-	Light Spear, Swordsmen	6	6-10	6-36
Javelin skirmishers	Light Foot	Unprotected	Average	Undrilled	Javelins	Light Spear	4	4-6	0-6

LATER SCOTS-IRISH

This list covers Irish (Scotti) armies from the later 5th century AD until the late 9th century when the Irish began to adopt Viking style weapons.

Ulster Warrior

TROOP NOTES

Most Irish warriors used very small shields, suitable only for parrying, but a larger shield was favoured in Ulster. All fought on foot, even if they arrived at the battlefield by chariot or on horseback.

Diberga and *Fianna* were members of pagan warrior cults. They shaved their hair at the front,

and grew it long and plaited at the back, adorned with "devilish tokens".

BUILDING A CUSTOMISED LIST USING OUR ARMY POINTS

Choose an army based on the maxima and minima in the list below. The following special instructions apply to this army:

- Commanders should be depicted as warriors.
- Irish allied commanders' contingents must conform to the Later Scots-Irish allies list below, but the troops in the contingent are deducted from the minima and maxima in the main list.
- Field fortifications can only be placed in Plantations or Forests.

Javelin Skirmisher

LATER SCOTS-IRISH										
Territory Types: Agricultural, Hilly, Woodlands										
C-in-C		Inspired Commander/Field Commander/Troop Commander						80/50/35	1	
Sub-commanders		Field Commander						50	0-2	
		Troop Commander						35	0-3	
Irish allied commanders		Field Commander/Troop Commander						40/25	0-2	
Troop name		Troop Type				Capabilities		Points per base	Bases per BG	Total bases
		Type	Armour	Quality	Training	Shooting	Close Combat			
Core Troops										
Warriors	Ulster	Medium Foot	Protected	Average	Undrilled	-	Light Spear, Swordsmen	6	6-12	32-208
	Rest of Ireland	Medium Foot	Unprotected	Average	Undrilled	-	Light Spear, Swordsmen	5		
Javelin skirmishers		Light Foot	Unprotected	Average	Undrilled	Javelins	Light Spear	4	6-8	6-24
Optional Troops										
Diberga and Fianna		Medium Foot	Unprotected	Superior	Undrilled	-	Impact Foot, Swordsmen	7	4-6	0-6
Slingers		Light Foot	Unprotected	Average	Undrilled	Sling	-	4	4	0-4
Barricades within woods		Field Fortifications							3	0-12
Allies										
British exile allies (Only from 680) – Post-Roman British										

LATER SCOTS-IRISH ALLIES										
Allied commander		Field Commander/Troop Commander						40/25	1	
Troop name		Troop Type				Capabilities		Points per base	Bases per BG	Total bases
		Type	Armour	Quality	Training	Shooting	Close Combat			
Warriors	Ulster	Medium Foot	Protected	Average	Undrilled	-	Light Spear, Swordsmen	6	6-12	8-36
	Rest of Ireland	Medium Foot	Unprotected	Average	Undrilled	-	Light Spear, Swordsmen	5		
Javelin skirmishers		Light Foot	Unprotected	Average	Undrilled	Javelins	Light Spear	4	4-8	4-8

MEROVINGIAN FRANKISH

In 486 AD, Clovis I, King of the Salian Franks and founder of the Merovingian dynasty, defeated Syagrius, "King" of a Roman rump-state in north-west modern France. In 496 he converted to Catholic Christianity. In 507 he defeated the Visigoths in southern France and forced them to retreat to their Iberian possessions. During his long reign he also conquered the Ripuarian Franks (on the Rhine) and the Alamanni, and reduced the Bretons to vassal status. At his death in 511, his rule extended over most of modern France and well into modern Germany.

On his death, as was the Frankish custom, his Kingdom was divided between his four sons, Chlothar I in Soissons, Childebert I in Paris, Chlodomer in Orleans and Theuderic I in Rheims. During their reigns, the Thuringians (532), Burgundi (534), and Saxons and Frisians (c.560) were conquered and incorporated into the Frankish kingdoms.

In 558 the Kingdom was (briefly) reunited under Chlothar I, but on his death in 561, it was divided again between his four sons. Fratricidal civil war followed, and this was the pattern in succeeding generations. The main divisions of Francia came to be Neustria (northern France), Austrasia (Germany), Burgundy (south-east France) and Aquitaine (south-west France).

Frankish Javelinman

By the end of the 7th century, the kings of the Merovingian dynasty were largely puppets, real power being held by successive Mayors of the Palace. Under the rule of Charles Martel (the Hammer), Mayor of the Palace of both Austrasia (from 714) and Neustria (from 717), the Frankish kingdoms were reunited. In 732 he led the army that defeated the invading Arabs at the Battle of Tours. In the past this victory has been credited with ending the threat of an Arab conquest of the whole of Europe. His son Pepin the Short, Mayor of the Palace of Neustria (from 741) and Austrasia (from 747), was crowned King of the Franks in 751. The last puppet Merovingian, Childeric III, was deposed and forced to enter a monastery.

This list covers Frankish armies from 496 until 751.

(Note: This list was referred to as "Middle Frankish" in earlier Field of Glory Companions).

TROOP NOTES

An earlier skirmishing style of cavalry combat seems to have been replaced c.600 by the fierce charge for which the Franks became famous. By then infantry of tribal or Gallo-Roman descent were probably indistinguishable from each other, and had adopted a shield-wall style of combat – see page 5.

Merovingian forces raid a Muslim camp, by Graham Turner. Taken from Campaign 190: Poitiers AD 732.

MEROVINGIAN FRANKISH STARTER ARMY (BEFORE 600 AD)		
Commander-in-Chief	1	Field Commander
Sub-commanders	2	2 x Troop Commander
Cavalry	2 BGs	Each comprising 4 bases of cavalry: Superior, Armoured, Undrilled Cavalry – Light Spear, Swordsmen
Cavalry	2 BGs	Each comprising 4 bases of cavalry: Superior, Protected, Undrilled Cavalry – Light Spear, Swordsmen
Frankish warriors	2 BGs	Each comprising 8 bases of Frankish warriors: Average, Protected, Undrilled Heavy Foot – Impact Foot, Swordsmen
Gallo-Roman spearmen	2 BGs	Each comprising 8 bases of Gallo-Roman spearmen: Average, Protected, Undrilled Heavy Foot – Light Spear, Swordsmen
Archers	1 BG	6 bases of archers: Average, Unprotected, Undrilled Light Foot – Bow
Javelinmen	1 BG	4 bases of javelinmen: Average, Unprotected, Undrilled Light Foot – Javelins, Light Spear
Camp	1	Unfortified camp
Total	10 BGs	Camp, 16 mounted bases, 42 foot bases, 3 commanders

BUILDING A CUSTOMISED LIST USING OUR ARMY POINTS

Choose an army based on the maxima and minima in the list below. The following special instructions apply to this army:

- Commanders should be depicted as cavalry.
- Cavalry (not light horse) can always dismount as Heavy Foot, Armoured or Protected (as mounted type), Superior, Undrilled, Impact Foot, Swordsmen (before 600) or Offensive Spearmen (from 600).
- Frankish allied commanders' contingents must conform to the Merovingian Frankish allies list below, but the troops in the contingent are deducted from the minima and maxima in the main list.

Gallo-Roman Spearman

MEROVINGIAN FRANKISH

Territory Types: Agricultural, Woodlands

C-in-C	Inspired Commander/Field Commander/Troop Commander	80/50/35	1
Sub-commanders	Field Commander	50	0-2
	Troop Commander	35	0-3
Frankish allied commanders	Field Commander/Troop Commander	40/25	0-2

Troop name		Troop Type: Type	Armour	Quality	Training	Capabilities: Shooting	Close Combat	Points per base	Bases per BG	Total bases	
Core Troops											
Frankish, Gallo-Roman, Alamannic or Burgundian cavalry	Only before 600	Cavalry	Armoured	Superior	Undrilled	-	Light Spear, Swordsmen	16	4-6	4-24	
			Armoured	Average				12			
			Protected	Superior				12			
			Protected	Average				9			
	Only from 600	Cavalry	Armoured	Superior	Undrilled	-	Lancers, Swordsmen	16	4-6		
			Armoured	Average				12			
			Protected	Superior				12			
			Protected	Average				9			
Frankish, Alamannic, Burgundian, Saxon or Thuringian warriors	Only before 600	Heavy Foot	Protected	Average	Undrilled	-	Impact Foot, Swordsmen	7	8-12	0-100	24-100
Gallo-Roman spearmen	Only before 600	Heavy Foot	Protected	Average	Undrilled	-	Light Spear, Swordsmen	6	6-8	0-100	
				Poor				4			
Spearmen	Only from 600	Heavy Foot	Protected	Average	Undrilled	-	Offensive Spearmen	7	6-8	24-100	
				Poor				5			
Optional Troops											
Foot archers		Light Foot	Unprotected	Average	Undrilled	Bow	-	5	6-8	0-8	
Javelinmen		Light Foot	Unprotected	Average	Undrilled	Javelins	Light Spear	4	4-6	0-6	
Alan, Breton or Thuringian cavalry		Cavalry	Armoured	Superior	Undrilled	-	Light Spear, Swordsmen	16	4	0-4	
			Armoured	Average				12			
			Protected	Superior				12			
			Protected	Average				9			
Breton or Basque cavalry		Light Horse	Unprotected	Average	Undrilled	Javelins	Light Spear	7	4	0-4	
Barricades		Field Fortifications						3		0-12	
Allies											
Breton allies											
Burgundian allies (Only before 532) – Early Frankish, Alamanni, Burgundi, Limigantes, Quadi, Rugii, Suebi or Turciling – See Field of Glory Companion 5: *Legions Triumphant: Imperial Rome at War*											
Visigothic allies (Only from 589) – Later Visigothic – See Field of Glory Companion 7: *Decline and Fall: Byzantium at War*											

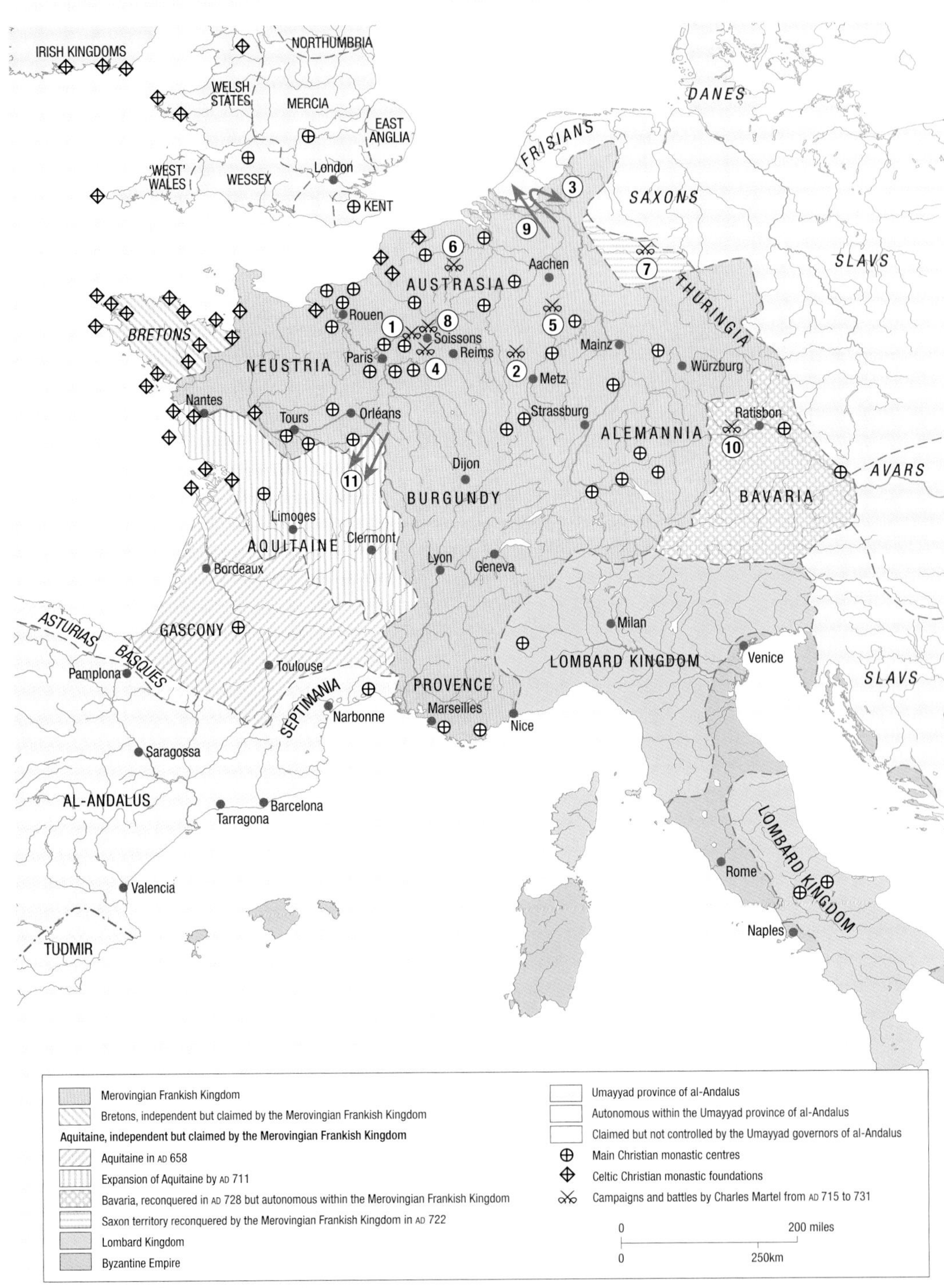

The Merovingian Frankish Kingdom and Charles Martel's campaigns, 715–731 AD. Taken from Campaign 190: Poitiers AD 732.

MEROVINGIAN FRANKISH ALLIES											
Allied commander		Field Commander/Troop Commander						40/25	1		
Troop name		**Troop Type**				**Capabilities**		**Points per base**	**Bases per BG**	**Total bases**	
		Type	Armour	Quality	Training	Shooting	Close Combat				
Core Troops											
Frankish, Gallo-Roman, Alamannic or Burgundian cavalry	Only before 600	Cavalry	Armoured	Superior	Undrilled	-	Light Spear, Swordsmen	16	4-6	0-8	
			Armoured	Average				12			
			Protected	Superior				12			
			Protected	Average				9			
	Only from 600	Cavalry	Armoured	Superior	Undrilled	-	Lancers, Swordsmen	16	4-6		
			Armoured	Average				12			
			Protected	Superior				12			
			Protected	Average				9			
Frankish, Alamannic, Burgundian, Saxon or Thuringian warriors	Only before 600	Heavy Foot	Protected	Average	Undrilled	-	Impact Foot, Swordsmen	7	8-12	0-32	8-32
Gallo-Roman spearmen	Only before 600	Heavy Foot	Protected	Average	Undrilled	-	Light Spear, Swordsmen	6	6-8	0-32	
				Poor				4			
Spearmen	Only from 600	Heavy Foot	Protected	Average	Undrilled	-	Offensive Spearmen	7	6-8	8-32	
				Poor				5			

BRETON ALLIES

This list covers allied contingents supplied by the Bretons from the later 6th century until the destruction of the Breton Kingdom by the Vikings circa 931. The new Duchy of Brittany created by a Breton counter-invasion from England in 936 adopted the Norman military system.

TROOP NOTES

Breton cavalry are described in Carolingian sources as javelin-armed skirmishers. Regino of Prüm, writing in the early 10th century, says the Bretons do not charge home but hurl javelins then swerve away after each attack. This is the last extant description of Bretons using such a fighting style.

- Commanders should be depicted as cavalry.

BRETON ALLIES										
Allied commander	Field Commander/Troop Commander						40/25	1		
Troop name	**Troop Type**				**Capabilities**		**Points per base**	**Bases per BG**	**Total bases**	
	Type	Armour	Quality	Training	Shooting	Close Combat				
Cavalry	Cavalry	Armoured	Superior	Undrilled	-	Light Spear, Swordsmen	16	4-6	0-8	4-16
	Cavalry	Protected	Superior	Undrilled	-	Light Spear, Swordsmen	12	4-6	0-16	
			Average				9			
	Light Horse	Unprotected	Average	Undrilled	Javelins	Light Spear	7	4-6	0-16	

INTRODUCTION
POST-ROMAN BRITISH
EARLY WELSH
LATER SCOTS-IRISH
MEROVINGIAN FRANKISH
BRETON ALLIES
LATER PICTISH
EARLY SLAVIC
MIDDLE ANGLO-SAXON
ASTUR-LEONESE
ANDALUSIAN
EARLY NAVARRESE
CAROLINGIAN FRANKISH
LOMBARD ALLIES
VIKING
MAGYAR
GREAT MORAVIAN
EARLY SCOTS
RUS
NORSE-IRISH
EARLY MEDIEVAL FRENCH
EARLY MEDIEVAL GERMAN
NORMAN
EARLY POLISH
ANGLO-DANISH
APPENDIX 1 - USING THE LISTS
APPENDIX 2 – THEMED TOURNAMENTS

Pictish infantry repelling Strathclyde cavalry, by Wayne Reynolds. Taken from Warrior 50: Pictish Warrior AD 297–841.

LATER PICTISH

This list covers Pictish armies from the beginning of the 6th century AD until the middle of the 9th century, when traditionally the Picts and Scots were united by Kenneth MacAlpin (Cináed mac Ailpín).

Pictish Light Horse

TROOP NOTES

Pictish shields seem to have become less flimsy during this period.

BUILDING A CUSTOMISED LIST USING OUR ARMY POINTS

Choose an army based on the maxima and minima in the list below. The following special instructions apply to this army:

- Commanders should be depicted as cavalry.

<table>
<tr><th colspan="11">LATER PICTISH</th></tr>
<tr><td colspan="11">Territory Types: Hilly, Woodlands</td></tr>
<tr><td>C-in-C</td><td colspan="6">Inspired Commander/Field Commander/Troop Commander</td><td>80/50/35</td><td colspan="3">1</td></tr>
<tr><td rowspan="2">Sub-commanders</td><td colspan="6">Field Commander</td><td>50</td><td colspan="3">0-2</td></tr>
<tr><td colspan="6">Troop Commander</td><td>35</td><td colspan="3">0-3</td></tr>
<tr><th rowspan="2">Troop name</th><th colspan="4">Troop Type</th><th colspan="2">Capabilities</th><th rowspan="2">Points per base</th><th rowspan="2">Bases per BG</th><th rowspan="2" colspan="2">Total bases</th></tr>
<tr><td>Type</td><td>Armour</td><td>Quality</td><td>Training</td><td>Shooting</td><td>Close Combat</td></tr>
<tr><th colspan="11">Core Troops</th></tr>
<tr><td rowspan="2">Cavalry</td><td>Cavalry</td><td>Protected</td><td>Average</td><td>Undrilled</td><td>-</td><td>Light Spear, Swordsmen</td><td>9</td><td>4</td><td>0-4</td><td rowspan="2">4-16</td></tr>
<tr><td>Light Horse</td><td>Unprotected</td><td>Average</td><td>Undrilled</td><td>Javelins</td><td>Light Spear</td><td>7</td><td>4-6</td><td>4-16</td></tr>
<tr><td rowspan="2">Spearmen</td><td rowspan="2">Medium Foot</td><td>Protected</td><td rowspan="2">Average</td><td rowspan="2">Undrilled</td><td rowspan="2">-</td><td rowspan="2">Offensive Spearmen</td><td>7</td><td rowspan="2">8-10</td><td rowspan="2" colspan="2">30-128</td></tr>
<tr><td>Unprotected</td><td>6</td></tr>
<tr><td>Archers</td><td>Light Foot</td><td>Unprotected</td><td>Average</td><td>Undrilled</td><td>Bow</td><td>-</td><td>5</td><td>6-8</td><td colspan="2">0-16</td></tr>
<tr><th colspan="11">Optional Troops</th></tr>
<tr><td>Javelinmen</td><td>Light Foot</td><td>Unprotected</td><td>Average</td><td>Undrilled</td><td>Javelins</td><td>Light Spear</td><td>4</td><td>6-8</td><td colspan="2">0-16</td></tr>
<tr><th colspan="11">Allies</th></tr>
<tr><td colspan="11">Scots-Irish allies – Later Scots-Irish</td></tr>
</table>

EARLY SLAVIC

This list covers Slavic armies in Northern, Central and Eastern Europe from the early 6th century AD until the foundation of Great Moravia in 833.

TROOP NOTES

Early Slavic armies fought mainly on foot with javelins. They were effective fighters in hilly or wooded country, and were fond of ambushes. They were vulnerable to cavalry charges in the open.

Slavic Warrior

Horse archery was adopted for part of the period under Avar influence. It dropped out of use again after the demise of the Avar Empire, and we assume that Slavic cavalry never developed the full expertise of their mentors.

BUILDING A CUSTOMISED LIST USING OUR ARMY POINTS

Choose an army based on the maxima and minima in the list below. The following special instructions apply to this army:

- Commanders should be depicted as cavalry.

<table>
<tr><th colspan="11">EARLY SLAVIC</th></tr>
<tr><td colspan="11">Territory Types: Hilly, Woodlands</td></tr>
<tr><td>C-in-C</td><td colspan="6">Inspired Commander/Field Commander/Troop Commander</td><td>80/50/35</td><td colspan="3">1</td></tr>
<tr><td rowspan="2">Sub-commanders</td><td colspan="6">Field Commander</td><td>50</td><td colspan="3">0-2</td></tr>
<tr><td colspan="6">Troop Commander</td><td>35</td><td colspan="3">0-3</td></tr>
<tr><td rowspan="2">Troop name</td><td colspan="4">Troop Type</td><td colspan="2">Capabilities</td><td rowspan="2">Points per base</td><td rowspan="2">Bases per BG</td><td rowspan="2" colspan="2">Total bases</td></tr>
<tr><td>Type</td><td>Armour</td><td>Quality</td><td>Training</td><td>Shooting</td><td>Close Combat</td></tr>
<tr><td colspan="11">Core Troops</td></tr>
<tr><td rowspan="6">Cavalry</td><td>Cavalry</td><td>Armoured</td><td>Superior</td><td>Undrilled</td><td>-</td><td>Light Spear, Swordsmen</td><td>16</td><td rowspan="2">4</td><td rowspan="2">0-4</td><td rowspan="6">0-12</td></tr>
<tr><td>Cavalry</td><td>Armoured</td><td>Superior</td><td>Undrilled</td><td>-</td><td>Light Spear, Bow*, Swordsmen</td><td>18</td></tr>
<tr><td rowspan="2">Cavalry</td><td rowspan="2">Protected</td><td>Superior</td><td rowspan="2">Undrilled</td><td rowspan="2">-</td><td rowspan="2">Light Spear, Swordsmen</td><td>12</td><td rowspan="2">4-6</td><td rowspan="4">0-12</td></tr>
<tr><td>Average</td><td>9</td></tr>
<tr><td rowspan="2">Cavalry</td><td rowspan="2">Protected</td><td>Superior</td><td rowspan="2">Undrilled</td><td rowspan="2"></td><td rowspan="2">Light Spear, Bow*, Swordsmen</td><td>14</td><td rowspan="2">4-6</td></tr>
<tr><td>Average</td><td>11</td></tr>
<tr><td>Foot warriors</td><td>Medium Foot</td><td>Protected</td><td>Average</td><td>Undrilled</td><td>-</td><td>Light Spear</td><td>5</td><td>6-8</td><td colspan="2">32-154</td></tr>
<tr><td>Archers</td><td>Light Foot</td><td>Unprotected</td><td>Average</td><td>Undrilled</td><td>Bow</td><td>-</td><td>5</td><td>6-8</td><td colspan="2">0-16</td></tr>
<tr><td colspan="11">Optional Troops</td></tr>
<tr><td>Skirmishing javelinmen</td><td>Light Foot</td><td>Unprotected</td><td>Average</td><td>Undrilled</td><td>Javelins</td><td>Light Spear</td><td>4</td><td>6-8</td><td colspan="2">0-16</td></tr>
<tr><td>Poorly armed foot</td><td>Medium Foot</td><td>Unprotected</td><td>Poor</td><td>Undrilled</td><td>-</td><td>Light Spear</td><td>2</td><td>10-12</td><td colspan="2">0-36</td></tr>
<tr><td colspan="11">Allies</td></tr>
<tr><td colspan="11">Bavarian or Old Saxon allies - Early Anglo-Saxon, Bavarian, Frisian, Old Saxon or Thuringian – See Field of Glory Companion 5: Legions Triumphant: Imperial Rome at War</td></tr>
</table>

<table>
<tr><th colspan="10">EARLY SLAVIC ALLIES</th></tr>
<tr><td>Allied commander</td><td colspan="6">Field Commander/Troop Commander</td><td>40/25</td><td colspan="2">1</td></tr>
<tr><td rowspan="2">Troop name</td><td colspan="4">Troop Type</td><td colspan="2">Capabilities</td><td rowspan="2">Points per base</td><td rowspan="2">Bases per BG</td><td rowspan="2">Total bases</td></tr>
<tr><td>Type</td><td>Armour</td><td>Quality</td><td>Training</td><td>Shooting</td><td>Close Combat</td></tr>
<tr><td rowspan="4">Cavalry</td><td rowspan="2">Cavalry</td><td rowspan="2">Protected</td><td>Superior</td><td rowspan="2">Undrilled</td><td rowspan="2">-</td><td rowspan="2">Light Spear, Swordsmen</td><td>12</td><td rowspan="2">4</td><td rowspan="4">0-4</td></tr>
<tr><td>Average</td><td>9</td></tr>
<tr><td rowspan="2">Cavalry</td><td rowspan="2">Protected</td><td>Superior</td><td rowspan="2">Undrilled</td><td rowspan="2">-</td><td rowspan="2">Light Spear, Bow*, Swordsmen</td><td>14</td><td rowspan="2">4</td></tr>
<tr><td>Average</td><td>11</td></tr>
<tr><td>Foot warriors</td><td>Medium Foot</td><td>Protected</td><td>Average</td><td>Undrilled</td><td>-</td><td>Light Spear</td><td>5</td><td>6-8</td><td>8-32</td></tr>
<tr><td>Archers</td><td>Light Foot</td><td>Unprotected</td><td>Average</td><td>Undrilled</td><td>Bow</td><td>-</td><td>5</td><td>4-6</td><td>0-6</td></tr>
<tr><td>Skirmishing javelinmen</td><td>Light Foot</td><td>Unprotected</td><td>Average</td><td>Undrilled</td><td>Javelins</td><td>Light Spear</td><td>4</td><td>4-6</td><td>0-6</td></tr>
</table>

MIDDLE ANGLO-SAXON

By the early 7th century AD, Anglo-Saxon England had stabilised into a number of kingdoms, conventionally known as the Heptarchy because the country was supposedly divided into the seven independent kingdoms of Northumbria, Mercia, East Anglia, Kent, Wessex, Essex and Sussex. However, it is doubtful whether Essex and Sussex ever achieved the same status as the others, and at various times there were other kingdoms or sub-kingdoms such as

Bernicia and Deira within Northumbria, Hwicce in the south-west Midlands, Magonsaete in Herefordshire, Lindsey in Lincolnshire and Middle Anglia in Leicestershire.

In the 7th and 8th centuries power shifted back and forth between the larger kingdoms. Christianity was adopted, the last pagan king, Penda of Mercia, dying in 655.

The first chronicled Viking raid on Britain was at Lindisfarne in 793. Danish settlement started in 865 when a large army of Danish Vikings under the brothers Halfdan Ragnarsson and Ivar the Boneless wintered in East Anglia. In 867 they captured York and conquered Northumbria, placing a puppet English king on the throne. King Æthelred of Wessex and his brother, Alfred (later King Alfred the Great), counterattacked with their army, meeting the Danes at Nottingham. The Danes, however, remained safely behind their fortifications and no battle occurred. King Burgred of Mercia then made peace with them, recognising their rule over the area around Nottingham in return for them leaving the rest of Mercia alone.

In 870 the Danes defeated and killed King Edmund of East Anglia and conquered that kingdom. Æthelred and Alfred attacked again, at Reading, but were defeated. The following January, however, they defeated the Danes at Ashdown. This, however, was followed by further English defeats at Basing in Hampshire and Marton in Wiltshire. Later that year, King Æthelred died and Alfred succeeded him as King of Wessex. His army was weak and he was forced to pay tribute to the Danes to gain peace. This, however, left the Danes free to continue their conquest of Mercia. War broke out again with Guthrum in command of the Danes, and by the winter of 877 Alfred was forced into hiding at Athelney in the marshland of the Somerset Levels. In 878, however, he gathered a new army, defeated the Danes at Chippenham, and forced Guthrum to accept peace and Christianity. After a further Danish defeat in 884, the area of the Danelaw (the area controlled by the Danes) was permanently fixed – comprising the whole of England north of a line drawn from London to Chester, excluding eastern Northumbria.

In 1013 King Sweyn Forkbeard of Denmark invaded England. The English King, Æthelred the

Anglo-Saxon Commander and Hirdsmen

INTRODUCTION
POST-ROMAN BRITISH
EARLY WELSH
LATER SCOTS-IRISH
MEROVINGIAN FRANKISH
BRETON ALLIES
LATER PICTISH
EARLY SLAVIC
MIDDLE ANGLO-SAXON
ASTUR-LEONESE
ANDALUSIAN
EARLY NAVARRESE
CAROLINGIAN FRANKISH
LOMBARD ALLIES
VIKING
MAGYAR
GREAT MORAVIAN
EARLY SCOTS
RUS
NORSE-IRISH
EARLY MEDIEVAL FRENCH
EARLY MEDIEVAL GERMAN
NORMAN
EARLY POLISH
ANGLO-DANISH
APPENDIX 1 - USING THE LISTS
APPENDIX 2 – THEMED TOURNAMENTS

The Battle of Winwaed, 655 AD, by Gerry Embleton. Taken from Warrior 5: Anglo-Saxon Thegn AD 449–1066.

Unready, fled to Normandy and Sweyn was accepted as King of England by the Witan and crowned on Christmas Day. In February of 1014, however, he died. His army elected his younger son Canute (Knut) as King of England, but then withdrew to Denmark. King Æthelred returned to England and was restored to the throne. In 1015, Canute reinvaded and by the end of 1016 was in control of the whole of England.

This list covers Anglo-Saxon armies from the early 7th century until the completion of the Danish conquest in 1016.

TROOP NOTES

The standard Anglo-Saxon battle formation was the shieldwall (*bord-weal* or *scyld-burh*) much as described under the Viking list, though less use was made of axes and archery. Mail coats were initially rare, but became more common later in the period.

The conventional view is that the Anglo-Saxons nearly always fought on foot. Recent academic thinking, however, has challenged this "received wisdom", for which there is in fact little evidence. Although there are only a few accounts specifically stating that troops fought mounted, accounts stating that they fought on foot are also uncommon. Thus for most recorded battles we don't know whether troops fought on foot or mounted. There is, by contrast, much evidence for the importance of the horse in Anglo-Saxon warfare. Those interested in exploring the subject further are referred to Guy Halsall's *Warfare and Society in the Barbarian West*, 450-900.

MIDDLE ANGLO-SAXON STARTER ARMY (AFTER 950 AD)		
Commander-in-Chief	1	Field Commander
Sub-commanders	2	2 x Troop Commander
Hirdsmen	2 BGs	Each comprising 8 bases of hirdsmen: Superior, Armoured, Undrilled Heavy Foot – Offensive Spearmen
Good quality fyrd	3 BGs	Each comprising 8 bases of good quality fyrd: Average, Protected, Undrilled Heavy Foot – Offensive Spearmen
Poor quality fyrd	2 BGs	Each comprising 8 bases of good quality fyrd: Poor, Protected, Undrilled Heavy Foot – Offensive Spearmen
Slingers	1 BG	6 bases of slingers: Average, Unprotected, Undrilled Light Foot – Sling
Javelinmen	1 BG	4 bases of javelinmen: Average, Unprotected, Undrilled Light Foot – Javelins, Light Spear
Camp	1	Unfortified camp
Total	9 BGs	Camp, 66 foot bases, 3 commanders

BUILDING A CUSTOMISED LIST USING OUR ARMY POINTS

Choose an army based on the maxima and minima in the list below. The following special instructions apply to this army:

- Commanders should be depicted as hirdsmen.
- Hirdsmen listed as Cavalry can always dismount as Heavy Foot, Protected or Armoured (as per their mounted type), Superior, Undrilled, Offensive Spearmen.
- Anglo-Saxon allied commanders' contingents must conform to the Middle Anglo-Saxon allies list below, but the troops in the contingent are deducted from the minima and maxima in the main list.

Poor Quality Fyrdman

Anglo-Saxon King, by Angus McBride. Taken from Men-at-Arms 154:
Arthur and the Anglo-Saxon Wars.

MIDDLE ANGLO-SAXON

Territory Types: Agricultural, Woodlands

C-in-C	Inspired Commander/Field Commander/Troop Commander	80/50/35	1
Sub-commanders	Field Commander	50	0-2
	Troop Commander	35	0-3
Anglo-Saxon allied commanders	Field Commander/Troop Commander	40/25	0-2

Troop name		Troop Type: Type	Armour	Quality	Training	Capabilities: Shooting	Close Combat	Points per base	Bases per BG	Total bases
Core Troops										
Hirdsmen	Any date	Heavy Foot	Protected	Superior	Undrilled	-	Offensive Spearmen	9	6-8	6-18
		Cavalry	Protected	Superior	Undrilled	-	Light Spear, Swordsmen	12	4-6	
	Only from 950	Heavy Foot	Armoured	Superior	Undrilled	-	Offensive Spearmen	12	6-8	
		Cavalry	Armoured	Superior	Undrilled	-	Light Spear, Swordsmen	16	4-6	
Good quality fyrd		Heavy Foot	Protected	Average	Undrilled	-	Offensive Spearmen	7	6-8	24-48
Poor quality fyrd		Heavy Foot	Protected	Poor	Undrilled	-	Offensive Spearmen	5	8-10	0-112
		Mob	Unprotected	Poor	Undrilled	-	-	2	8-12	0-20
Optional Troops										
Vassal British cavalry	Only before 700	Cavalry	Protected	Average	Undrilled	-	Light Spear, Swordsmen	9	4	0-4
				Superior				12		
Archers		Light Foot	Unprotected	Average	Undrilled	Bow	-	5	4-6	0-6
Slingers		Light Foot	Unprotected	Average	Undrilled	Sling	-	4	4-6	0-6, 0-12
Javelinmen		Light Foot	Unprotected	Average	Undrilled	Javelins	Light Spear	4	4-6	0-6
Allies										
Welsh allies (Only before 700) – Early Welsh										
Viking allies (Only from 1012)										

MIDDLE ANGLO-SAXON ALLIES

Allied commander	Field Commander/Troop Commander	40/25	1

Troop name		Troop Type: Type	Armour	Quality	Training	Capabilities: Shooting	Close Combat	Points per base	Bases per BG	Total bases
Hirdsmen	Any date	Heavy Foot	Protected	Superior	Undrilled	-	Offensive Spearmen	9	4-6	0-6
		Cavalry	Protected	Superior	Undrilled	-	Light Spear, Swordsmen	12	4-6	
	Only from 950	Heavy Foot	Armoured	Superior	Undrilled	-	Offensive Spearmen	12	4-6	
		Cavalry	Armoured	Superior	Undrilled	-	Light Spear, Swordsmen	16	4-6	
Good quality fyrd		Heavy Foot	Protected	Average	Undrilled	-	Offensive Spearmen	7	6-8	6-16
Poor quality fyrd		Heavy Foot	Protected	Poor	Undrilled	-	Offensive Spearmen	5	8-10	0-24
Archers		Light Foot	Unprotected	Average	Undrilled	Bow	-	5	4	0-4
Slingers		Light Foot	Unprotected	Average	Undrilled	Sling	-	4	4	
Javelinmen		Light Foot	Unprotected	Average	Undrilled	Javelins	Light Spear	4	4	

ASTUR-LEONESE

Don Pelayo, the first Asturian king, was a former member of the Visigothic court in Toledo who found shelter in the Cantabrian Mountains after the Umayyad invasion of the Iberian Peninsula. From there he began the Reconquista, leading local forces and Visigothic troops who had maintained resistance to the invading Moslems in the mountains.

During the 9th and 10th centuries AD, the Astur-Leonese kingdom had to fight off several Viking raids and suffered from internal dynastic disputes, but nevertheless managed to maintain its southwards expansion.

In the early 11th century the kingdom was weakened by renewed internal conflicts, the attacks of the Andalusians led by Al-Mansur, and the expansionistic policy of Sancho III of Navarre, whose son Fernando I first became Count of Castile, then, after a short civil war, King of León and Castile.

This list covers Christian armies in the north west of modern Spain, from the founding of the Asturian kingdom in 718, through its conversion into the kingdom of León, until the death of Bermudo III in the battle of Tamarón in 1037 fighting against the Count of Castile, Fernando I.

Astur-Leonese Commander

TROOP NOTES

Early armies followed the Visigothic tradition, but with a very important presence of light infantry who could cope well with the rugged terrain of northern Spain. Later on, and as the kingdom expanded south and west, many Christian refugees fleeing from persecution in the areas under Muslim control provided additional forces, and the militias of the reconquered cities increased the importance of heavy infantry again.

Cavalry came from a number of groups: *Ricoshombres* were the higher nobility, descendants of the Visigothic and Hispano-Roman aristocracy. *Infanzones* were the lesser nobility. *Caballeros villanos* were rich burghers accepted as nobles from the mid 10th century.

Astur-Leonese Javelinman

ASTUR-LEONESE STARTER ARMY (BEFORE 900 AD)		
Commander-in-Chief	1	Field Commander
Sub-commanders	2	2 x Troop Commander
Noble cavalry	3 BGs	Each comprising 4 bases of noble cavalry: Superior, Armoured, Undrilled Cavalry – Lancers, Swordsmen
Noble cavalry	2 BGs	Each comprising 4 bases of noble cavalry: Superior, Protected, Undrilled Cavalry – Light Spear, Swordsmen
Spearmen	2 BGs	Each comprising 8 bases of Spearmen: Average, Protected, Undrilled Heavy Foot – Defensive Spearmen
Archers	1 BG	8 bases of archers: Average, Unprotected, Undrilled Light Foot – Bow
Javelinmen	1 BG	8 bases of javelinmen: Average, Unprotected, Undrilled Light Foot – Javelins, Light Spear
Slingers	1 BG	6 bases of slingers: Average, Unprotected, Undrilled Light Foot – Sling
Camp	1	Unfortified camp
Total	10 BGs	Camp, 20 mounted bases, 38 foot bases, 3 commanders

BUILDING A CUSTOMISED LIST USING OUR ARMY POINTS

- Commanders should be depicted as noble cavalry.

<table>
<tr><th colspan="13">ASTUR-LEONESE</th></tr>
<tr><td colspan="13">Territory Types: Agricultural, Developed, Hilly, Mountains</td></tr>
<tr><td colspan="2">C-in-C</td><td colspan="6">Inspired Commander/Field Commander/Troop Commander</td><td>80/50/35</td><td colspan="4">1</td></tr>
<tr><td colspan="2" rowspan="2">Sub-commanders</td><td colspan="6">Field Commander</td><td>50</td><td colspan="4">0-2</td></tr>
<tr><td colspan="6">Troop Commander</td><td>35</td><td colspan="4">0-3</td></tr>
<tr><td colspan="2" rowspan="2">Troop name</td><td colspan="4">Troop Type</td><td colspan="2">Capabilities</td><td rowspan="2">Points per base</td><td colspan="2" rowspan="2">Bases per BG</td><td colspan="2" rowspan="2">Total bases</td></tr>
<tr><td>Type</td><td>Armour</td><td>Quality</td><td>Training</td><td>Shooting</td><td>Close Combat</td></tr>
<tr><td colspan="13">Core Troops</td></tr>
<tr><td rowspan="3">Noble cavalry</td><td>Any date</td><td>Cavalry</td><td>Armoured</td><td>Superior</td><td>Undrilled</td><td>-</td><td>Lancers, Swordsmen</td><td>16</td><td colspan="2">4-6</td><td>8-32</td><td rowspan="3">8-32</td></tr>
<tr><td rowspan="2">Only before 900</td><td rowspan="2">Cavalry</td><td rowspan="2">Protected</td><td>Superior</td><td rowspan="2">Undrilled</td><td rowspan="2">-</td><td rowspan="2">Light Spear, Swordsmen</td><td>12</td><td colspan="2" rowspan="2">4-6</td><td rowspan="2">0-12</td></tr>
<tr><td>Average</td><td>9</td></tr>
<tr><td colspan="2">Spearmen</td><td>Heavy Foot</td><td>Protected</td><td>Average</td><td>Undrilled</td><td>-</td><td>Defensive Spearmen</td><td>6</td><td>2/3 or all</td><td rowspan="2">8-12</td><td colspan="2">8-36</td></tr>
<tr><td colspan="2">Supporting archers</td><td>Light Foot</td><td>Unprotected</td><td>Average</td><td>Undrilled</td><td>Bow</td><td>-</td><td>5</td><td>1/3 or 0</td><td>0-18</td><td rowspan="3">6-28</td></tr>
<tr><td colspan="2" rowspan="2">Separately deployed archers</td><td>Light Foot</td><td>Unprotected</td><td>Average</td><td>Undrilled</td><td>Bow</td><td>-</td><td>5</td><td colspan="2">6-8</td><td rowspan="2">0-18</td></tr>
<tr><td>Medium Foot</td><td>Unprotected</td><td>Average</td><td>Undrilled</td><td>Bow</td><td>-</td><td>5</td><td colspan="2">6-8</td></tr>
<tr><td colspan="2">Javelinmen</td><td>Light Foot</td><td>Unprotected</td><td>Average</td><td>Undrilled</td><td>Javelins</td><td>Light Spear</td><td>4</td><td colspan="2">6-8</td><td colspan="2">8-48</td></tr>
<tr><td colspan="13">Optional Troops</td></tr>
<tr><td colspan="2">Slingers</td><td>Light Foot</td><td>Unprotected</td><td>Average</td><td>Undrilled</td><td>Sling</td><td>-</td><td>4</td><td colspan="2">6-8</td><td colspan="2">0-12</td></tr>
<tr><td colspan="2">Basque or mercenary Berber light horse</td><td>Light Horse</td><td>Unprotected</td><td>Average</td><td>Undrilled</td><td>Javelins</td><td>Light Spear</td><td>7</td><td colspan="2">4-6</td><td colspan="2">0-6</td></tr>
<tr><td rowspan="2">Foot crossbowmen</td><td rowspan="2">Only from 950</td><td>Light Foot</td><td>Unprotected</td><td>Average</td><td>Undrilled</td><td>Crossbow</td><td>-</td><td>5</td><td colspan="2">6-8</td><td colspan="2" rowspan="2">0-8</td></tr>
<tr><td>Medium Foot</td><td>Unprotected</td><td>Average</td><td>Undrilled</td><td>Crossbow</td><td>-</td><td>5</td><td colspan="2">6-8</td></tr>
<tr><td colspan="2">Fortified camp</td><td></td><td></td><td></td><td></td><td></td><td></td><td>24</td><td colspan="2"></td><td colspan="2">0-1</td></tr>
<tr><td colspan="13">Allies</td></tr>
<tr><td colspan="13">Navarrese allies (Only from 860) – Early Navarrese</td></tr>
</table>

<table>
<tr><th colspan="13">ASTUR-LEONESE ALLIES</th></tr>
<tr><td colspan="2">Allied commander</td><td colspan="6">Field Commander/Troop Commander</td><td>40/25</td><td colspan="4">1</td></tr>
<tr><td colspan="2" rowspan="2">Troop name</td><td colspan="4">Troop Type</td><td colspan="2">Capabilities</td><td rowspan="2">Points per base</td><td colspan="2" rowspan="2">Bases per BG</td><td colspan="2" rowspan="2">Total bases</td></tr>
<tr><td>Type</td><td>Armour</td><td>Quality</td><td>Training</td><td>Shooting</td><td>Close Combat</td></tr>
<tr><td rowspan="3">Noble cavalry</td><td>Any date</td><td>Cavalry</td><td>Armoured</td><td>Superior</td><td>Undrilled</td><td>-</td><td>Lancers, Swordsmen</td><td>16</td><td colspan="2">4-6</td><td>4-8</td><td rowspan="3">4-8</td></tr>
<tr><td rowspan="2">Only before 900</td><td rowspan="2">Cavalry</td><td rowspan="2">Protected</td><td>Superior</td><td rowspan="2">Undrilled</td><td rowspan="2">-</td><td rowspan="2">Light Spear, Swordsmen</td><td>12</td><td colspan="2" rowspan="2">4</td><td rowspan="2">0-4</td></tr>
<tr><td>Average</td><td>9</td></tr>
<tr><td colspan="2">Spearmen</td><td>Heavy Foot</td><td>Protected</td><td>Average</td><td>Undrilled</td><td>-</td><td>Defensive Spearmen</td><td>6</td><td>2/3 or all</td><td rowspan="2">8-12</td><td colspan="2">0-8</td></tr>
<tr><td colspan="2">Supporting archers</td><td>Light Foot</td><td>Unprotected</td><td>Average</td><td>Undrilled</td><td>Bow</td><td>-</td><td>5</td><td>1/3 or 0</td><td>0-4</td><td rowspan="3">0-8</td></tr>
<tr><td colspan="2" rowspan="2">Separately deployed archers</td><td>Light Foot</td><td>Unprotected</td><td>Average</td><td>Undrilled</td><td>Bow</td><td>-</td><td>5</td><td colspan="2">6-8</td><td rowspan="2">6-8</td></tr>
<tr><td>Medium Foot</td><td>Unprotected</td><td>Average</td><td>Undrilled</td><td>Bow</td><td>-</td><td>5</td><td colspan="2">6-8</td></tr>
<tr><td colspan="2">Javelinmen</td><td>Light Foot</td><td>Unprotected</td><td>Average</td><td>Undrilled</td><td>Javelins</td><td>Light Spear</td><td>4</td><td colspan="2">6-8</td><td colspan="2">0-12</td></tr>
</table>

INTRODUCTION
POST-ROMAN BRITISH
EARLY WELSH
LATER SCOTS-IRISH
MEROVINGIAN FRANKISH
BRETON ALLIES
LATER PICTISH
EARLY SLAVIC
MIDDLE ANGLO-SAXON
ASTUR-LEONESE
ANDALUSIAN
EARLY NAVARRESE
CAROLINGIAN FRANKISH
LOMBARD ALLIES
VIKING
MAGYAR
GREAT MORAVIAN
EARLY SCOTS
RUS
NORSE-IRISH
EARLY MEDIEVAL FRENCH
EARLY MEDIEVAL GERMAN
NORMAN
EARLY POLISH
ANGLO-DANISH
APPENDIX 1 - USING THE LISTS
APPENDIX 2 – THEMED TOURNAMENTS

ANDALUSIAN

This list covers Muslim armies of the Emirate (later Caliphate) of Cordoba from the arrival of the Umayyad dynasty in 755 AD until the abolition of the Andalusian Caliphate in 1031. Al-Andalus was the Arab name for the Muslim possessions in the Iberian peninsula (all but the far north of modern Spain and Portugal).

The Emirate of Cordoba was founded in 756 by Abd al-Rahman I, the last survivor of the Umayyad dynasty after the Abbasid revolution. Leading an army of Syrian Jund troops supported by North African Berber tribesmen, he ended the internal disputes between different Muslim factions that had afflicted Al-Andalus since the original invasion of 711, and established a centralised power independent from Baghdad with its capital at Cordoba.

In 929, in an attempt to reinforce central power again after a series of renewed internal conflicts, and following the example of the newly proclaimed Fatimid Caliphate in North Africa, Abd al-Rahman III declared himself a Caliph. He smashed all his opponents and converted Cordoba into the largest and richest city of Western Europe, in direct competition with Baghdad and Constantinople. He failed, however, to defeat the Christian kingdoms in the north.

At the end of the 10th century the Caliphate reached its maximum extent under the military dictatorship of the Hajib (Grand Vizier) Al-Mansur, who, in an attempt to weaken any internal opposition, clearly favoured his Berber and "Slav" troops at the expense of the Arabs and Syrians. Following his death in 1002, his son Abd al-Malik ruled until his own death in 1008. Another son, Abd al-Rahman, then attempted to seize the Caliphate for himself, but was assassinated in 1009. The Caliphate was then fragmented by civil war, encouraged by Christian interference (Castile supporting the Berber party and Catalonia supporting the "Slav" party), and was finally abolished in 1031. The Andalusian state was then divided into a number of small kingdoms called Taifa kingdoms. These are covered in a later volume.

TROOP NOTES

Syrian Jund troops took refuge in Spain after being defeated in the North African rebellions of 740.

At various times assorted guard units were raised from white or black slave recruits. The Hasham Guard or "Silent Ones" created by Hakam I in 770 was originally formed from Egyptian troops, but later came to consist of "Slav" mamluks (mixed European slave recruits). The "Slav Guard", created by Abd al-Rahman III in the early 10th century, fought with swords and were equipped with mail coats. The "Black Guard" was raised from black slave recruits. They swore an oath never to flee but to fight to the last man in defence of the Caliph.

Andalusian Spearman

Black Guard

Andalusian troops, by Angus McBride. Taken from Men-at-Arms 125: The Armies of Islam 7th–11th Centuries.

ANDALUSIAN STARTER ARMY		
Commander-in-Chief	1	Field Commander
Sub-commanders	2	2 x Troop Commander
Jund cavalry	2 BGs	Each comprising 4 bases of Jund cavalry: Superior, Armoured, Drilled Cavalry – Lancers, Swordsmen
Andalusian or Berber cavalry	3 BGs	Each comprising 4 bases of Andalusian or Berber light horse: Average, Unprotected, Undrilled Light Horse – Javelins, Light Spear
Black Guard	1 BG	Each comprising 8 bases of Black Guard: Superior, Protected, Drilled Heavy Foot – Defensive Spearmen
Andalusian regular spearmen	2 BGs	Each comprising 8 bases of Andalusian regular spearmen: Average, Protected, Drilled Heavy Foot – Defensive Spearmen
Archers	2 BGs	Each comprising 6 bases of archers: Average, Unprotected, Undrilled Light Foot – Bow
Slingers	1 BG	8 bases of slingers: Poor, Unprotected, Undrilled Light Foot - Sling
Camp	1	Unfortified camp
Total	11 BGs	Camp, 20 mounted bases, 44 foot bases, 3 commanders

BUILDING A CUSTOMISED LIST USING OUR ARMY POINTS

- Commanders should be depicted as Jund, Arab or Andalusian cavalry.
- The minimum marked * only applies before 1010.
- Minima marked ** apply if any foot are used.
- From 1009, Berbers and "Slav Guard" cannot be used together.
- Castilian allies cannot be used with the "Slav Guard" nor with Catalan allies
- Catalan allies cannot be used with Berbers nor with Castilian allies.

Black Spearman

ANDALUSIAN

Territory Types: Developed, Agricultural, Hilly

C-in-C	Inspired Commander/Field Commander/Troop Commander	80/50/35	1
Sub-commanders	Field Commander	50	0-2
	Troop Commander	35	0-3

Troop name		Type	Armour	Quality	Training	Shooting	Close Combat	Points per base	Bases per BG		Total bases	
Core Troops												
Jund or guard cavalry	Only before 1010	Cavalry	Armoured	Superior	Drilled	-	Lancers, Swordsmen	17	4-6		0-12	*4-18
			Armoured	Average				13				
			Protected	Superior				13				
			Protected	Average				10				
Other Arab Cavalry		Cavalry	Armoured	Superior	Undrilled	-	Lancers, Swordsmen	16	4-6		0-12	
			Armoured	Average				12				
			Protected	Superior				12				
			Protected	Average				9				
Andalusian or Berber cavalry		Light Horse	Unprotected	Average	Undrilled	Javelins	Light Spear	7	4-6		12-36	
Andalusian regular spearmen		Heavy Foot	Protected	Average	Drilled	-	Defensive Spearmen	7	2/3 or all	8-12	8-24	
Supporting archers		Light Foot	Unprotected	Average	Drilled	Bow	-	5	1/3 or 0		0-12	8-24
Separately deployed archers		Light Foot	Unprotected	Average	Drilled or Undrilled	Bow	-	5	6-8		0-24	
				Poor				3				
		Medium Foot	Unprotected	Average	Drilled	Bow	-	6	6-8			
Optional Troops												
"Black Guard"	Only before 978	Heavy Foot	Protected	Superior	Drilled	-	Defensive Spearmen	9	6-8		0-8	0-12
"Silent Ones"	Only from 770 to 928	Heavy Foot	Protected	Superior	Drilled	-	Defensive Spearmen	9	6-8		0-8	
				Average				7				
"Slav Guard"	Only from 929	Heavy Foot	Armoured	Superior	Drilled	-	Light Spear, Swordsmen	12	6-8		0-8	
Andalusian levy spearmen		Heavy Foot	Protected	Poor	Undrilled	-	Defensive Spearmen	4	2/3 or all	8-12	0-12	
Supporting archers		Light Foot	Unprotected	Poor	Undrilled	Bow	-	3	1/3 or 0		0-6	
Other black spearmen		Medium Foot	Protected	Average	Undrilled	-	Light Spear	5	6-8		0-8	
Slingers		Light Foot	Unprotected	Average	Drilled or Undrilled	Sling	-	4	6-8		0-8	
				Poor				2				
Berber javelinmen		Light Foot	Unprotected	Average	Undrilled	Javelins	Light Spear	4	6-8		0-40	
		Medium Foot	Protected	Average	Undrilled	-	Light Spear	5	6-8			
Horse archers		Light Horse	Unprotected	Average	Drilled	Bow	-	8	4		0-4	
Fortified camp								24			0-1	
Allies												
Castilian allies (Only from 1010) – Astur-Leonese												
Catalan allies (Only from 1010) – Catalan and Early Crown of Aragon – See Field of Glory Companion 10: *Oath of Fealty: Feudal Europe at War*												

<table>
<tr><th colspan="13">ANDALUSIAN ALLIES</th></tr>
<tr><td colspan="2">Allied commander</td><td colspan="6">Field Commander/Troop Commander</td><td>40/25</td><td colspan="4">1</td></tr>
<tr><th colspan="2" rowspan="2">Troop name</th><th colspan="4">Troop Type</th><th colspan="2">Capabilities</th><th rowspan="2">Points per base</th><th colspan="2" rowspan="2">Bases per BG</th><th colspan="2" rowspan="2">Total bases</th></tr>
<tr><th>Type</th><th>Armour</th><th>Quality</th><th>Training</th><th>Shooting</th><th>Close Combat</th></tr>
<tr><td rowspan="4">Jund or guard cavalry</td><td rowspan="4">Only before 1010</td><td rowspan="4">Cavalry</td><td>Armoured</td><td>Superior</td><td rowspan="4">Drilled</td><td rowspan="4">-</td><td rowspan="4">Lancers, Swordsmen</td><td>17</td><td colspan="2" rowspan="4">4-6</td><td colspan="2" rowspan="8">0-6</td></tr>
<tr><td>Armoured</td><td>Average</td><td>13</td></tr>
<tr><td>Protected</td><td>Superior</td><td>13</td></tr>
<tr><td>Protected</td><td>Average</td><td>10</td></tr>
<tr><td colspan="2" rowspan="4">Other Arab Cavalry</td><td rowspan="4">Cavalry</td><td>Armoured</td><td>Superior</td><td rowspan="4">Undrilled</td><td rowspan="4">-</td><td rowspan="4">Lancers, Swordsmen</td><td>16</td><td colspan="2" rowspan="4">4-6</td></tr>
<tr><td>Armoured</td><td>Average</td><td>12</td></tr>
<tr><td>Protected</td><td>Superior</td><td>12</td></tr>
<tr><td>Protected</td><td>Average</td><td>9</td></tr>
<tr><td colspan="2">Andalusian or Berber cavalry</td><td>Light Horse</td><td>Unprotected</td><td>Average</td><td>Undrilled</td><td>Javelins</td><td>Light Spear</td><td>7</td><td colspan="2">4-6</td><td colspan="2">4-12</td></tr>
<tr><td colspan="2">Andalusian regular spearmen</td><td>Heavy Foot</td><td>Protected</td><td>Average</td><td>Drilled</td><td>-</td><td>Defensive Spearmen</td><td>7</td><td>2/3 or all</td><td rowspan="2">8-12</td><td colspan="2">**6-8</td></tr>
<tr><td colspan="2">Supporting archers</td><td>Light Foot</td><td>Unprotected</td><td>Average</td><td>Drilled</td><td>Bow</td><td>-</td><td>5</td><td>1/3 or 0</td><td>0-4</td><td rowspan="4">**3-8</td></tr>
<tr><td colspan="2" rowspan="3">Separately deployed archers</td><td rowspan="2">Light Foot</td><td rowspan="2">Unprotected</td><td>Average</td><td rowspan="2">Drilled or Undrilled</td><td rowspan="2">Bow</td><td rowspan="2">-</td><td>5</td><td colspan="2" rowspan="2">6-8</td><td rowspan="3">0-8</td></tr>
<tr><td>Poor</td><td>3</td></tr>
<tr><td>Medium Foot</td><td>Unprotected</td><td>Average</td><td>Drilled</td><td>Bow</td><td>-</td><td>6</td><td colspan="2">6-8</td></tr>
<tr><td colspan="2" rowspan="2">Berber javelinmen</td><td>Light Foot</td><td>Unprotected</td><td>Average</td><td>Undrilled</td><td>Javelins</td><td>Light Spear</td><td>4</td><td colspan="2">6-8</td><td colspan="2" rowspan="2">0-12</td></tr>
<tr><td>Medium Foot</td><td>Protected</td><td>Average</td><td>Undrilled</td><td>-</td><td>Light Spear</td><td>5</td><td colspan="2">6-8</td></tr>
</table>

EARLY NAVARRESE

In the late 8th century AD, Charlemagne seized control over the Pyrenees in order to secure the southern border of his empire against the Muslims. In 778, retiring from a failed expedition against Saragossa, he destroyed Pamplona on the way back north as a punishment for Navarrese sympathies towards the Banu Qasi, a Muslim dynasty of Visigothic origin that ruled over the upper Ebro Valley. In revenge, the local troops ambushed the rearguard of the Frankish army a couple of days later at Roncesvalles, inflicting a severe defeat that inspired the famous *Chanson de Roland*.

Although the Franks nominally recovered control over Pamplona, this defeat was the beginning of the process that led to the independence of Navarre with the final expulsion of the Franks by the Andalusians with local support in 816, and the creation of the Kingdom of Pamplona in 824.

In 859 Viking raiders arrived at Pamplona after crossing the Ebro River unopposed by the Banu Qasi. They sacked the city and captured King García I. He returned to the city after payment of a hefty ransom, but from then on broke his alliance with the Banu Qasi, and instead allied himself with the Christian Astur-Leonese Kingdom.

Navarre reached its maximum expansion under Sancho III. Married to Munia, daughter of Sancho García, Count of Castile, he ruled over Castile after the murder of his father-in-law and conquered the capital of León in 1034. To the east, he took over the Counties of Aragon,

Ribagorza and Sobrarbe, formerly under nominal Frankish rule as part of the Hispanic March. At his death in 1035 he split his possessions between his four sons. Ramiro I received the County of Aragon, now converted into a brand new Kingdom. García Sánchez II became the new King of Navarre. Fernando inherited the County of Castile, and became King of León after a short civil war against Bermudo III. Gonzalo Sánchez received the Counties of Sobrarbe and Ribagorza, also converted into a Kingdom, but this was incorporated into Aragon at his death ten years later.

The list covers Navarrese armies from the insurrection against Charlemagne and the battle of Roncesvalles until the death of Sancho III.

TROOP NOTES

Early armies were composed mostly of light infantry, able to cope with the rugged landscape of the Navarrese Pyrenees. Later on, as the Kingdom expanded towards the rich Ebro valley, the militias of the reconquered cities supplied increasing numbers of heavy infantry.

The Navarrese nobility adopted Frankish heavy cavalry tactics.

EARLY NAVARRESE STARTER ARMY		
Commander-in-Chief	1	Field Commander
Sub-commanders	2	2 x Troop Commander
Noble cavalry	4 BGs	Each comprising 4 bases of noble cavalry: Superior, Armoured, Undrilled Cavalry – Lancers, Swordsmen
Basque cavalry	2 BGs	Each comprising 6 bases of Basque cavalry: Average, Unprotected, Undrilled Light Horse – Javelins, Light Spear
Archers	1 BG	8 bases of archers: Average, Unprotected, Undrilled Light Foot – Bow
Javelinmen	4 BGs	Each comprising 6 bases of javelinmen: Average, Unprotected, Undrilled Light Foot – Javelins, Light Spear
Camp	1	Unfortified camp
Total	10 BGs	Camp, 28 mounted bases, 32 foot bases, 3 commanders

BUILDING A CUSTOMISED LIST USING OUR ARMY POINTS

- Commanders should be depicted as noble cavalry.

Navarrese Spearman

EARLY NAVARRESE

Territory Types: Agricultural, Hilly, Mountains

Troop name		Type	Armour	Quality	Training	Shooting	Close Combat	Points per base	Bases per BG	Total bases
C-in-C		Inspired Commander/Field Commander/Troop Commander						80/50/35	1	
Sub-commanders		Field Commander						50	0-2	
		Troop Commander						35	0-3	
Core Troops										
Noble cavalry	Before 900	Cavalry	Armoured	Superior	Undrilled	-	Lancers, Swordsmen	16	4-6	4-18
	From 900									8-30
Javelinmen		Medium Foot	Protected	Average	Undrilled	-	Light Spear	5	6-8	16-96
			Unprotected					4		
		Light Foot	Unprotected	Average	Undrilled	Javelins	Light Spear	4	6-8	
Optional Troops										
Basque cavalry		Light Horse	Unprotected	Average	Undrilled	Javelins	Light Spear	7	4-6	0-18
Spearmen		Heavy Foot	Protected	Average	Undrilled	-	Defensive Spearmen	6	2/3 or all, 8-12	0-24
Supporting archers		Light Foot	Unprotected	Average	Undrilled	Bow	-	5	1/3 or 0	0-12
Separately deployed archers		Light Foot	Unprotected	Average	Undrilled	Bow	-	5	6-8	
		Medium Foot	Unprotected	Average	Undrilled	Bow	-	5	6-8	
Slingers		Light Foot	Unprotected	Average	Undrilled	Sling	-	4	6-8	0-18
Fortified camp								24		0-1
Allies										
Andalusian allies (Only before 860)										
Leonese allies – Astur-Leonese (Only from 860)										

EARLY NAVARRESE ALLIES

Troop name		Type	Armour	Quality	Training	Shooting	Close Combat	Points per base	Bases per BG	Total bases
Allied commander		Field Commander/Troop Commander						40/25	1	
Noble cavalry	Before 900	Cavalry	Armoured	Superior	Undrilled	-	Lancers, Swordsmen	16	4-6	4-6
	From 900									4-10
Javelinmen		Medium Foot	Protected	Average	Undrilled	-	Light Spear	5	6-8	6-24
			Unprotected					4		
		Light Foot	Unprotected	Average	Undrilled	Javelins	Light Spear	4	6-8	
Basque cavalry		Light Horse	Unprotected	Average	Undrilled	Javelins	Light Spear	7	4-6	0-6
Spearmen		Heavy Foot	Protected	Average	Undrilled	-	Defensive Spearmen	6	2/3 or all, 8-12	0-8
Supporting archers		Light Foot	Unprotected	Average	Undrilled	Bow	-	5	1/3 or 0	0-4
Separately deployed archers		Light Foot	Unprotected	Average	Undrilled	Bow	-	5	4	
		Medium Foot	Unprotected	Average	Undrilled	Bow	-	5	4	
Slingers		Light Foot	Unprotected	Average	Undrilled	Sling	-	4	4	0-4

CAROLINGIAN FRANKISH

In 751 Pepin the Short was crowned King of the Franks, the first king of the Carolingian dynasty. In 759 he drove the Arabs out of southern France and annexed Aquitaine. In 768 he died, and was succeeded by his sons Charles (Charlemagne) and Carloman.

Carloman died suddenly in 771, leaving Charlemagne as sole king. During his reign, which lasted 46 years, he conquered the Lombard kingdom in northern Italy (774), Saxony (777–797), Bavaria and Carinthia (788). In 778 he conquered a strip of northern Spain, but failed to conquer the rest of the Iberian peninsula from the Muslims. Beyond the eastern frontiers of his Empire, he forced the Avars and various Slavic peoples to accept vassal status. In 800 he was crowned "Emperor of the Romans" by Pope Leo III.

Charlemagne died in 814, his son Louis the Pious succeeding him as Emperor. The later years of Louis' reign were plagued by civil war between him and his sons. Louis died in 840, and in 843 the Empire was partitioned between his sons by the Treaty of Verdun. Lothar became Emperor and King of Middle Francia – comprising Italy, Burgundy, Provence and western Austrasia. Louis the German became King of East Francia – the rest of modern Germany. This realm was the precursor to the Holy Roman Empire. Charles the Bald became King of West Francia – the rest of modern France.

Gascon Cavalryman

Further subdivisions and civil wars occurred, but by 884, Charlemagne's empire was reunited again under Charles the Fat. However, partly due to the depredations of Viking raiders, he was unable to hold it together, was deposed in 887 and died in exile in 888.

Following his death the Carolingian Empire was finally divided: Count Odo of Paris became King of West Francia (France); Arnulf of Carinthia, an illegitimate Carolingian, became King of East Francia (Germany); Duke Ranulf II of Aquitaine became King of Aquitaine; Margrave Berengar of Friuli became King of Italy; Rudolph I became King of Upper Burgundy and Louis the Blind King of Lower Burgundy.

This list covers Frankish armies from 751 until 888.

TROOP NOTES

By this time cavalry had become the decisive arm. West Frankish cavalry were renowned among their contemporaries for the fierceness of their charge, but were also willing to dismount and fight on foot when necessary. East Frankish cavalry sometimes used feigned flight, and often preferred to fight on foot.

Cavalry battle groups are treated as Armoured or Protected depending on the proportion of men with mail coats.

Carolingian troops in the field, by Angus McBride. Taken from Men-at-Arms 150: The Age of Charlemagne.

CAROLINGIAN FRANKISH STARTER ARMY		
Commander-in-Chief	1	Inspired Commander (Charlemagne)
Sub-commanders	2	2 x Troop Commander
Imperial retainers	2 BGs	Each comprising 4 bases of Imperial retainers: Superior, Armoured, Drilled Cavalry – Lancers, Swordsmen
West Frankish cavalry	1 BG	4 bases of West Frankish cavalry: Superior, Armoured, Undrilled Cavalry – Lancers, Swordsmen
East Frankish cavalry	2 BGs	Each comprising 4 bases of East Frankish cavalry: Superior, Protected, Undrilled Cavalry – Light Spear, Swordsmen
Gascon cavalry	1 BG	4 bases of Gascon cavalry: Average, Unprotected, Undrilled Light Horse – Javelins, Light Spear
Spearmen	2 BGs	Each comprising 8 bases of Spearmen: Average, Protected, Undrilled Heavy Foot – Defensive Spearmen
Archers	1 BG	6 bases of archers: Average, Unprotected, Undrilled Light Foot – Bow
Camp	1	Unfortified camp
Total	9 BGs	Camp, 24 mounted bases, 22 foot bases, 3 commanders

BUILDING A CUSTOMISED LIST USING OUR ARMY POINTS

Choose an army based on the maxima and minima in the list below. The following special instructions apply to this army:

- Commanders should be depicted as cavalry.
- Imperial retainers can always dismount as Heavy Foot, Armoured, Superior, Drilled, Offensive Spearmen.
- West or East Frankish cavalry can always dismount as Heavy Foot, Armoured or Protected (as mounted type), Superior, Undrilled, Offensive Spearmen.
- Frankish "horse archers" can always dismount as Medium Foot, Armoured, Superior, Drilled or Undrilled (as per their mounted type), Bow, Swordsmen.
- Gascon, Basque or Andalusian troops cannot be used with East Franks or Croatians.
- Breton cavalry from the Optional Troops list cannot be used with Breton allies.
- Frankish allied commanders' contingents must conform to the Carolingian Frankish allies list below, but the troops in the contingent are deducted from the minima and maxima in the main list.
- Only one non-Frankish allied contingent can be used.

CAROLINGIAN FRANKISH											
Territory Types: Agricultural, Woodlands											
C-in-C		Inspired Commander/Field Commander/Troop Commander						80/50/35	1		
Sub-commanders		Field Commander						50	0-2		
		Troop Commander						35	0-3		
Frankish allied commanders		Field Commander/Troop Commander						40/25	0-2		
Troop name		Troop Type				Capabilities		Points per base	Bases per BG	Total bases	
		Type	Armour	Quality	Training	Shooting	Close Combat				
Core Troops											
Imperial retainers	Only from 768 to 814	Cavalry	Armoured	Superior	Drilled	-	Lancers, Swordsmen	17	4-6	0-18	12-48
West Frankish cavalry		Cavalry	Armoured	Superior	Undrilled	-	Lancers, Swordsmen	16	4-6	0-48	
			Protected					12			
East Frankish cavalry		Cavalry	Armoured	Superior	Undrilled	-	Lancers, Swordsmen	16	4-6	0-18	
			Armoured	Average				12			
			Protected	Superior				12			
			Protected	Average				9			
		Cavalry	Armoured	Superior	Undrilled	-	Light Spear, Swordsmen	16	4-6	0-8	
			Armoured	Average				12			
			Protected	Superior				12			
			Protected	Average				9			
Frankish "horse archers"	Only from 768 to 814	Cavalry	Armoured	Average	Undrilled	-	Lancers, Swordsmen	16	4	0-4	
				Drilled				17			
Spearmen		Heavy Foot	Protected	Average	Undrilled	-	Defensive Spearmen	6	2/3 or all	8-9	8-48
Supporting archers		Light Foot	Unprotected	Average	Undrilled	Bow	-	5	1/3 or 0		
Optional Troops											
Separately deployed foot archers		Light Foot	Unprotected	Average	Undrilled	Bow	-	5	4-6	0-6	
		Medium Foot	Unprotected	Average	Undrilled	Bow	-	5	4-6		
Gascon or Basque javelinmen		Light Foot	Unprotected	Average	Undrilled	Javelins	Light Spear	4	4-6	0-6	
Gascon, Basque or Andalusian cavalry		Light Horse	Unprotected	Average	Undrilled	Javelins	Light Spear	7	4	0-4	
Breton cavalry		Cavalry	Armoured	Superior	Undrilled	-	Light Spear, Swordsmen	16	4	0-4	
			Armoured	Average				12			
			Protected	Superior				12			
			Protected	Average				9			
Peasants		Mob	Unprotected	Poor	Undrilled	-	-	2	8-12	0-12	
Fortified camp								24		0-1	
Allies											
Breton allies											
Croatian allies (Only from 799) – Early South Slav – See Field of Glory Companion 7: *Decline and Fall: Byzantium at War*											
Frisian or Old Saxon allies (Only from 716 to 804) – Early Anglo-Saxon, Bavarian, Frisian, Old Saxon or Thuringian – See Field of Glory Companion 5: *Legions Triumphant: Imperial Rome at War*											
Lombard subject allies (Only from 774)											
Viking allies (Only from 857)											
Western Slav subject allies (Only from 790) – Early Slavic											

CAROLINGIAN FRANKISH ALLIES												
Allied commander		Field Commander/Troop Commander						40/25	1			
Troop name		Troop Type				Capabilities		Points per base	Bases per BG		Total bases	
		Type	Armour	Quality	Training	Shooting	Close Combat					
Imperial retainers	Only from 768 to 814	Cavalry	Armoured	Superior	Drilled	-	Lancers, Swordsmen	17	4		0-4	4-12
West Frankish cavalry		Cavalry	Armoured	Superior	Undrilled	-	Lancers, Swordsmen	16	4-6		0-12	
			Protected					12				
East Frankish cavalry		Cavalry	Armoured	Superior	Undrilled	-	Lancers, Swordsmen	16	4-6		0-6	
			Armoured	Average				12				
			Protected	Superior				12				
			Protected	Average				9				
		Cavalry	Armoured	Superior	Undrilled	-	Light Spear, Swordsmen	16	4		0-4	
			Armoured	Average				12				
			Protected	Superior				12				
			Protected	Average				9				
Spearmen		Heavy Foot	Protected	Average	Undrilled	-	Defensive Spearmen	6	2/3 or all	8-9	8-9	
Supporting archers		Light Foot	Unprotected	Average	Undrilled	Bow	-	5	1/3 or 0			

LOMBARD ALLIES

This list covers allied contingents from the independent Lombard duchies following the Frankish conquest of the Lombard Kingdom. (See *Field of Glory Companion 7: Decline and Fall*).

- Commanders should be depicted as armoured cavalry.

LOMBARD ALLIES									
Allied commander	Field Commander/Troop Commander						40/25	1	
Troop name	Troop Type				Capabilities		Points per base	Bases per BG	Total bases
	Type	Armour	Quality	Training	Shooting	Close Combat			
Armoured cavalry	Cavalry	Armoured	Superior	Undrilled	-	Lancers, Swordsmen	16	4-6	4-12
Archers	Medium Foot	Unprotected	Average	Undrilled	Bow	-	5	4-6	0-6
			Poor				3		
	Light Foot	Unprotected	Average	Undrilled	Bow	-	5	4-6	
			Poor				3		
Italian militias	Heavy Foot	Protected	Poor	Undrilled	-	Defensive Spearmen	4	6-8	0-8
				Drilled			5		

Carolingian troops ambush a Viking raiding party, by Wayne Reynolds. Taken from Warrior 96: Carolingian Cavalryman AD 768–987.

VIKING

From the late 8th century AD the Scandinavian peoples of Denmark, Norway and Sweden erupted forth from their homeland in their famous longships as raiders, merchants, invaders and settlers. Their travels took them as far afield as Russia and Constantinople in the East, Spain and North Africa in the South and Newfoundland in the West. Their raids terrorized the coastal areas of Western Europe and often probed far up the larger rivers. Their settlements played a major role in the history of England, Scotland, Ireland and Russia, as described in the notes for the relevant lists. Viking settlers in France became the Normans, who had a major part to play in English, French and Italian history and the First Crusade.

The term Viking comes from Old Norse *vikingr* ("one who came from the fjords").

This list covers Danish, Norwegian and Swedish armies at home and overseas from the late 8th century until the development of knightly cavalry in the later 12th century. It does not cover Rus armies, which have their own list.

TROOP NOTES

The standard Viking battlefield formation was the shieldwall (*skjaldborg*), comprising men armed with various combinations of sword, axe, throwing spears and thrusting spears. This

The Battle of Hafrsfjord, 872 *AD*, by Gerry Embleton. Taken from *Warrior* 3: Viking Hersir 793–1066 AD.

The North Sea countries c. 1066. *Taken from Essential Histories 12:* Campaigns of the Norman Conquest.

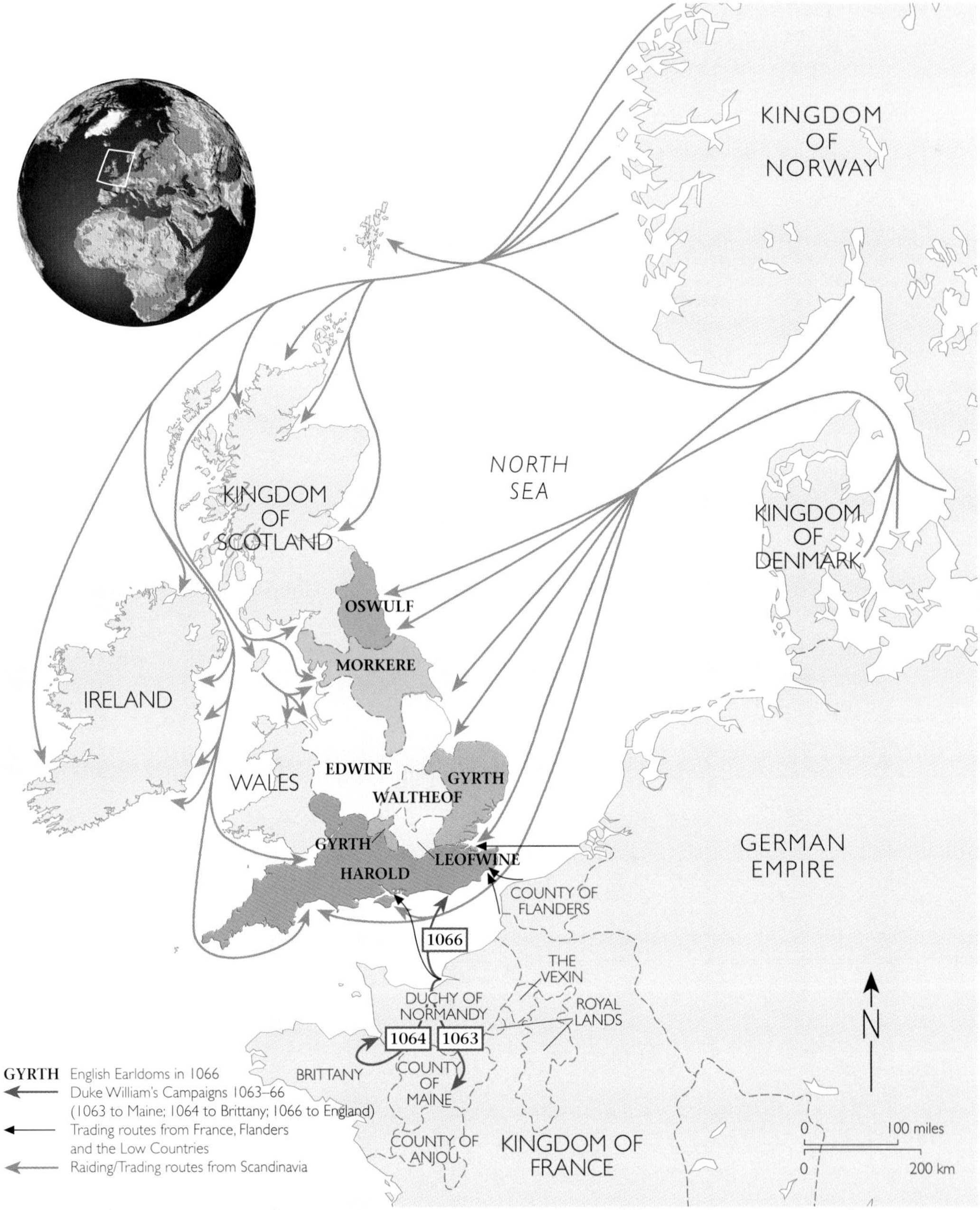
KINGDOM OF NORWAY
NORTH SEA
KINGDOM OF SCOTLAND
KINGDOM OF DENMARK
OSWULF
MORKERE
IRELAND
WALES
EDWINE
GYRTH
WALTHEOF
GYRTH
LEOFWINE
HAROLD
GERMAN EMPIRE
COUNTY OF FLANDERS
1066
THE VEXIN
DUCHY OF NORMANDY
ROYAL LANDS
1064
1063
BRITTANY
COUNTY OF MAINE
COUNTY OF ANJOU
KINGDOM OF FRANCE
N
0
100 miles
0
200 km
GYRTH English Earldoms in 1066
Duke William's Campaigns 1063–66
(1063 to Maine; 1064 to Brittany; 1066 to England)
Trading routes from France, Flanders
and the Low Countries
Raiding/Trading routes from Scandinavia

Viking Shieldwall

formation is best represented under the rules as Offensive Spearmen. Archers would form up in the rear ranks. They can be represented separately as supporting light foot, or assumed to be included in the overall effect of the shieldwall.

The famous two-handed Viking axe came into use from about 900. Battle groups with Heavy Weapon capability are those with a high proportion of men armed with two-handed axe.

Berserkers, while they certainly existed, were not present in large enough numbers to form separate battle groups.

Vikings often rode to battle on horses, but usually dismounted to fight.

BUILDING A CUSTOMISED LIST USING OUR ARMY POINTS

Choose an army based on the maxima and minima in the list below. The following special instructions apply to this army:

- Commanders should be depicted as huscarls.
- Mounted huscarls can always dismount as Heavy Foot, Armoured, Superior, Undrilled, Offensive Spearmen.

Viking Commander

DUBLIN VIKING STARTER ARMY (AFTER 900 AD)		
Commander-in-Chief	1	Field Commander
Sub-commanders	2	2 x Troop Commander
Huscarls	2 BGs	Each comprising 8 bases of huscarls: Superior, Armoured, Undrilled Heavy Foot – Heavy Weapon
Freemen	3 BGs	Each comprising 8 bases of freemen: Average, Protected, Undrilled Heavy Foot – Offensive Spearmen
Irish	1 BG	8 bases of Irish: Average, Unprotected, Undrilled Medium Foot – Heavy Weapon
Archers	1 BG	6 bases of archers: Average, Unprotected, Undrilled Light Foot – Bow
Thralls	1 BG	8 bases of thralls: Poor, Unprotected, Undrilled Mob – no capabilities
Camp	1	Fortified camp
Total	8 BGs	Fortified camp, 62 foot bases, 3 commanders

Vikings clash at sea, by Angus McBride. Taken from Elite 3: The Vikings.

VIKING

Territory Types: Agricultural, Woodlands, Hilly, Mountains

C-in-C		Inspired Commander/Field Commander/Troop Commander						80/50/35	1		
Sub-commanders		Field Commander						50	0-2		
		Troop Commander						35	0-3		
Troop name		**Troop Type**				**Capabilities**		**Points per base**	**Bases per BG**		**Total bases**
		Type	Armour	Quality	Training	Shooting	Close Combat				
Core Troops											
Huscarls	Any date	Heavy Foot	Armoured	Superior	Undrilled	-	Offensive Spearmen	12	2/3 or all	6-9	6-18
	Only from 900	Heavy Foot	Armoured	Superior	Undrilled	-	Heavy Weapon	12			
Supporting archers		Light Foot	Unprotected	Superior	Undrilled	Bow	-	6	1/3 or 0		0-9
Freemen		Heavy Foot	Protected	Average	Undrilled	-	Offensive Spearmen	7	2/3 or all	8-9	24-92
Supporting archers		Light Foot	Unprotected	Average	Undrilled	Bow	-	5	1/3 or 0		0-46
Optional Troops											
Upgrade huscarls to		Cavalry	Armoured	Superior	Undrilled	-	Light Spear, Swordsmen	16	4-6		0-12
Separately deployed archers		Light Foot	Unprotected	Average	Undrilled	Bow	-	5	6-8		0-8
Thralls		Mob	Unprotected	Poor	Undrilled	-	-	2	6-8		0-8
Irish	Only in Ireland	Medium Foot	Unprotected	Average	Undrilled	-	Light Spear, Swordsmen	5	6-8		0-12
		Light Foot	Unprotected	Average	Undrilled	Javelins	Light Spear	4			
	Only in Ireland from 900	Medium Foot	Unprotected	Average	Undrilled	-	Heavy Weapon	6	6-8		
Fortified Camp								24			0-1

Allies
Breton allies (Only in France in 866)
Cornish allies (Only in Britain from 838 to 900) – Post-Roman British
English rebel allies (Only in Britain in 1066 or 1069)
Frankish allies (Only in France from 857 to 922) – Carolingian Frankish or Early Medieval French
Irish allies (Only in Ireland) – Norse-Irish
Scots allies (Only in Britain in 1069) – Feudal Scots – See Field of Glory Companion 10: *Oath of Fealty: Feudal Europe at War*

VIKING ALLIES

Allied commander		Field Commander/Troop Commander						40/25	1		
Troop name		**Troop Type**				**Capabilities**		**Points per base**	**Bases per BG**		**Total bases**
		Type	Armour	Quality	Training	Shooting	Close Combat				
Huscarls	Any date	Heavy Foot	Armoured	Superior	Undrilled	-	Offensive Spearmen	12	2/3 or all	6-9	0-8
	Only from 900	Heavy Foot	Armoured	Superior	Undrilled	-	Heavy Weapon	12			
Supporting archers		Light Foot	Unprotected	Superior	Undrilled	Bow	-	6	1/3 or 0		0-3
Upgrade huscarls to		Cavalry	Armoured	Superior	Undrilled	-	Light Spear, Swordsmen	16	4-6		0-6
Freemen		Heavy Foot	Protected	Average	Undrilled	-	Offensive Spearmen	7	2/3 or all	8-9	8-24
Supporting archers		Light Foot	Unprotected	Average	Undrilled	Bow	-	5	1/3 or 0		0-12

Viking raiders, by Angus McBride. Taken from Elite 3: The Vikings.

MAGYAR

The Finno-Ugrian Magyars erupted into European history in the 9th century AD. Prior to 830 they lived around the Don River south west of the Ural mountains in modern Russia, subject to the Khazar Khaganate (See *Field of Glory Companion 7: Decline and Fall*). Following a civil war in the Khaganate (or possibly as a result of attacks by the Pechenegs), three Kabar tribes of the Khazars joined the Magyars and the combined horde migrated west to the modern Ukraine between the Carpathians and the Dnieper River. From 862 they launched a series of raids against the Eastern Frankish (German) Empire, Great Moravia and Bulgaria.

In the 890s, probably as a result of attacks by the Bulgarians and the Pechenegs, they moved under their leader Árpád into the Carpathian basin (modern Hungary and Romania). From there they continued their raids across continental Europe, defeating German armies at Pressburg (907) and Augsburg (910), and plundering Alsace, Basle, Burgundy, Provence and Saxony. They overran much of the Slovakian territory of Great Moravia by 925.

The Magyar defeat by the Germans at Lechfeld in 955 ended their threat to Western Europe, although they continued to raid the Balkans until 970. In 1000 their High Prince, Vajk, accepted Christianity. He was recognised as King of Hungary by Pope Sylvester II and ruled under his Christian name of István (Stephen) I.

This list covers Magyar armies from 830 until 1000.

Magyar Heavy Cavalry

TROOP NOTES

Magyar armies consisted almost entirely of mounted horse archers. Even after their conquest of the Carpathian basin they made little use of their Slav subjects as troops.

Géza, father of István I, introduced a bodyguard of Bavarian knights, to whom he granted large estates.

Magyar Light Cavalry

MAGYAR STARTER ARMY		
Commander-in-Chief	1	Field Commander
Sub-commanders	2	2 x Troop Commander
Heavy cavalry	3 BGs	Each comprising 4 bases of heavy cavalry: Superior, Armoured, Undrilled Cavalry – Bow, Swordsmen
Light cavalry	6 BGs	Each comprising 4 bases of light cavalry: Average, Unprotected, Undrilled Light Horse – Bow, Swordsmen
Slav levy archers	1 BG	8 bases of Slav archers: Poor, Unprotected, Undrilled Light Foot – Bow
Camp	1	Unfortified camp
Total	10 BGs	Fortified camp, 36 mounted bases, 8 foot bases, 3 commanders

BUILDING A CUSTOMISED LIST USING OUR ARMY POINTS

Choose an army based on the maxima and minima in the list below. The following special instructions apply to this army:

- Commanders should be depicted as heavy cavalry.

MAGYAR									
Territory Types: Steppes, Agricultural									
C-in-C	Inspired Commander/Field Commander/Troop Commander						80/50/35	1	
Sub-commanders	Field Commander						50	0-2	
	Troop Commander						35	0-3	
Troop name	Troop Type				Capabilities		Points per base	Bases per BG	Total bases
	Type	Armour	Quality	Training	Shooting	Close Combat			
Core Troops									
Armoured cavalry	Cavalry	Armoured	Superior	Undrilled	Bow	Swordsmen	18	4-6	0-20
Light cavalry	Light Horse	Unprotected	Average	Undrilled	Bow	Swordsmen	10	4-6	20-80
	Cavalry	Unprotected	Average	Undrilled	Bow	Swordsmen	10		
		Protected					11		
Optional Troops									
Slav or other levy foot	Heavy Foot	Protected	Average	Undrilled	-	Defensive Spearmen	6	6-8	0-8
			Poor				4		
	Medium Foot	Protected	Average	Undrilled	-	Light Spear	5	6-8	
			Poor				3		
	Light foot	Unprotected	Average	Undrilled	Bow	-	5	6-8	
			Poor				3		
	Mob	Unprotected	Poor	Undrilled	-	-	2	6-8	
Bavarian bodyguard (Only from 975)	Cavalry	Armoured	Superior	Undrilled	-	Lancers. Swordsmen	16	4	0-4
			Average				12		
Fortified camp (wagon laager)							24		0-1

MAGYAR ALLIES									
Allied commander	Field Commander/Troop Commander						40/25	1	
Troop name	Troop Type				Capabilities		Points per base	Bases per BG	Total bases
	Type	Armour	Quality	Training	Shooting	Close Combat			
Armoured cavalry	Cavalry	Armoured	Superior	Undrilled	Bow	Swordsmen	18	4-6	0-6
Light cavalry	Light Horse	Unprotected	Average	Undrilled	Bow	Swordsmen	10	4-6	6-24
	Cavalry	Unprotected	Average	Undrilled	Bow	Swordsmen	10		
		Protected					11		

Magyar cavalryman, by Angus McBride. Taken from Men-at-Arms 333: Armies of Medieval Russia 750–1250.

GREAT MORAVIAN

Founded by Prince Mojmír I in 833, the Great Moravian Empire was a Slavic state in Central Europe. At its greatest extent, under King Svätopluk I (871–894), it included modern Slovakia and the Czech Republic as well as parts of Austria, Germany, Hungary, Romania, Poland, Serbia, Slovenia, Croatia and Ukraine. Weakened by war with the Kingdom of Germany (Eastern Francia) and internal dynastic disputes, it was overrun by the Magyars in the early 10th century.

The allies list also covers contingents supplied by Slavic successor entities such as Bohemia under the Přemyslid dynasty.

Moravian Commander

GREAT MORAVIAN STARTER ARMY		
Commander-in-Chief	1	Field Commander
Sub-commanders	2	2 x Troop Commander
Cavalry	2 BGs	Each comprising 4 bases of cavalry: Superior, Armoured, Undrilled Cavalry – Light Spear, Swordsmen
Cavalry	2 BGs	Each comprising 4 bases of cavalry: Average, Protected, Undrilled Cavalry – Light Spear, Swordsmen
Spearmen	4 BGs	Each comprising 8 bases of spearmen: Average, Protected, Undrilled Heavy Foot – Defensive Spearmen
Archers	2 BGs	Each comprising 8 bases of peasant archers: Average, Unprotected, Undrilled Light Foot – Bow
Camp	1	Unfortified camp
Total	10 BGs	Camp, 16 mounted bases, 48 foot bases, 3 commanders

BUILDING A CUSTOMISED LIST USING OUR ARMY POINTS

Choose an army based on the maxima and minima in the list below. The following special instructions apply to this army:

- Commanders should be depicted as cavalry.
- Only one allied contingent can be used.

Frankish Cavalryman

<table>
<tr><th colspan="11">GREAT MORAVIAN</th></tr>
<tr><td colspan="11">Territory Types: Agricultural, Hilly, Woodlands</td></tr>
<tr><td>C-in-C</td><td colspan="6">Inspired Commander/Field Commander/Troop Commander</td><td>80/50/35</td><td colspan="3">1</td></tr>
<tr><td rowspan="2">Sub-commanders</td><td colspan="6">Field Commander</td><td>50</td><td colspan="3">0-2</td></tr>
<tr><td colspan="6">Troop Commander</td><td>35</td><td colspan="3">0-3</td></tr>
<tr><td rowspan="2">Troop name</td><td colspan="4">Troop Type</td><td colspan="2">Capabilities</td><td rowspan="2">Points per base</td><td rowspan="2">Bases per BG</td><td colspan="2" rowspan="2">Total bases</td></tr>
<tr><td>Type</td><td>Armour</td><td>Quality</td><td>Training</td><td>Shooting</td><td>Close Combat</td></tr>
<tr><td colspan="11">Core Troops</td></tr>
<tr><td rowspan="3">Cavalry</td><td rowspan="2">Cavalry</td><td>Armoured</td><td rowspan="2">Superior</td><td rowspan="2">Undrilled</td><td rowspan="2">-</td><td rowspan="2">Light Spear, Swordsmen</td><td>16</td><td rowspan="2">4-6</td><td rowspan="2">0-8</td><td rowspan="3">4-16</td></tr>
<tr><td>Protected</td><td>12</td></tr>
<tr><td>Cavalry</td><td>Protected</td><td>Average</td><td>Undrilled</td><td>-</td><td>Light Spear, Swordsmen</td><td>9</td><td>4-6</td><td>0-12</td></tr>
<tr><td>Spearmen</td><td>Heavy Foot</td><td>Protected</td><td>Average</td><td>Undrilled</td><td>-</td><td>Defensive Spearmen</td><td>6</td><td>6-8</td><td colspan="2">24-124</td></tr>
<tr><td rowspan="2">Archers</td><td>Light Foot</td><td>Unprotected</td><td>Average</td><td>Undrilled</td><td>Bow</td><td>-</td><td>5</td><td>6-8</td><td colspan="2" rowspan="2">6-24</td></tr>
<tr><td>Medium Foot</td><td>Unprotected</td><td>Average</td><td>Undrilled</td><td>Bow</td><td>-</td><td>5</td><td>6-8</td></tr>
<tr><td colspan="11">Optional Troops</td></tr>
<tr><td rowspan="4">Frankish cavalry</td><td rowspan="4">Cavalry</td><td>Armoured</td><td>Superior</td><td rowspan="4">Undrilled</td><td rowspan="4">-</td><td rowspan="4">Lancers, Swordsmen</td><td>16</td><td rowspan="4">4</td><td colspan="2" rowspan="4">0-4</td></tr>
<tr><td>Armoured</td><td>Average</td><td>12</td></tr>
<tr><td>Protected</td><td>Superior</td><td>12</td></tr>
<tr><td>Protected</td><td>Average</td><td>9</td></tr>
<tr><td rowspan="2">Horse archers</td><td>Light Horse</td><td>Unprotected</td><td>Average</td><td>Undrilled</td><td>Bow</td><td>Swordsmen</td><td>10</td><td rowspan="2">4</td><td colspan="2" rowspan="2">0-4</td></tr>
<tr><td>Light Horse</td><td>Unprotected</td><td>Average</td><td>Undrilled</td><td>Bow</td><td>-</td><td>8</td></tr>
<tr><td colspan="11">Allies</td></tr>
<tr><td colspan="11">East Frankish allies – Early Medieval German</td></tr>
<tr><td colspan="11">Magyar allies</td></tr>
<tr><td colspan="11">Pecheneg allies – See Field of Glory Companion 7: Decline and Fall: Byzantium at War</td></tr>
</table>

GREAT MORAVIAN ALLIES										
Allied commander	Field Commander/Troop Commander						40/25	1		
Troop name	Troop Type				Capabilities		Points per base	Bases per BG	Total bases	
	Type	Armour	Quality	Training	Shooting	Close Combat				
Cavalry	Cavalry	Armoured	Superior	Undrilled	-	Light Spear, Swordsmen	16	4	0-4	4-6
		Protected					12			
	Cavalry	Protected	Average	Undrilled	-	Light Spear, Swordsmen	9	4-6	0-6	
Spearmen	Heavy Foot	Protected	Average	Undrilled	-	Defensive Spearmen	6	6-8	6-24	
Archers	Light Foot	Unprotected	Average	Undrilled	Bow	-	5	6-8	0-8	
	Medium Foot	Unprotected	Average	Undrilled	Bow	-	5	6-8		

EARLY SCOTS

Traditionally, the Picts and Scots were united by Kenneth MacAlpin (Cináed mac Ailpín) in the middle of the 9th century AD, but this tradition was developed some considerable time after the events. It was his grandson Constantine II (Constantín mac Áeda) who was the first recorded King of Alba (Scotland), from c.900. Initially the kingdom only ruled north of the Forth and Clyde rivers. The south-west of modern Scotland was the British Kingdom of Strathclyde and the south-east was the English Kingdom of Bernicia, a sub-kingdom of Northumberland. Moreover, in the north and west, Caithness, Sutherland and the Western Isles were in the hands of the Viking Jarls of Orkney.

Bernicia may have been ceded to Scotland by the English King Edgar the Peaceful in 973, but was certainly Scottish after their victory at Carham-on-Tweed in 1018. Strathclyde was conquered some time between 1019 and 1053.

This list covers Scottish armies from the mid-9th century until 1052, when Macbeth gave a number of Norman exiles from England refuge at his court.

Thegn

EARLY SCOTS STARTER ARMY		
Commander-in-Chief	1	Field Commander
Sub-commanders	2	2 x Troop Commander
Cavalry	1 BG	4 bases of cavalry: Average, Armoured, Undrilled Cavalry – Light Spear, Swordsmen
Cavalry	1 BG	4 bases of cavalry: Average, Unprotected, Undrilled Light Horse – Javelins, Light Spear
Thegns	2 BGs	Each comprising 6 bases of thegns: Superior, Armoured, Undrilled Heavy Foot – Impact Foot, Swordsmen
Spearmen	4 BGs	Each comprising 8 bases of spearmen: Average, Protected, Undrilled Medium Foot – Offensive Spearmen
Archers	1 BG	6 bases of archers: Average, Unprotected, Undrilled Light Foot – Bow
Camp	1	Unfortified camp
Total	9 BGs	Camp, 8 mounted bases, 50 foot bases, 3 commanders

BUILDING A CUSTOMISED LIST USING OUR ARMY POINTS

Choose an army based on the maxima and minima in the list below. The following special instructions apply to this army:

- Commanders should be depicted as cavalry.
- Thegns must all be classified the same.

EARLY SCOTS

Territory Types: Hilly, Woodlands										
C-in-C	Inspired Commander/Field Commander/Troop Commander						80/50/35	1		
Sub-commanders	Field Commander						50	0-2		
	Troop Commander						35	0-3		
Troop name	Troop Type				Capabilities		Points per base	Bases per BG	Total bases	
	Type	Armour	Quality	Training	Shooting	Close Combat				
Core Troops										
Cavalry	Cavalry	Armoured	Average	Undrilled	-	Light Spear, Swordsmen	12	4	0-4	4-16
	Cavalry	Protected	Average	Undrilled	-	Light Spear, Swordsmen	9	4-6	0-8	
	Light Horse	Unprotected	Average	Undrilled	Javelins	Light Spear	7	4-6	0-12	
Thegns	Heavy Foot	Armoured	Superior	Undrilled	-	Impact Foot, Swordsmen	12	6-8	6-12	
		Protected					9			
	Heavy Foot	Armoured	Superior	Undrilled	-	Offensive Spearmen	12	6-8		
		Protected					9			
Spearmen	Medium Foot	Protected	Average	Undrilled	-	Offensive Spearmen	7	8-10	20-104	
Archers	Light Foot	Unprotected	Average	Undrilled	Bow	-	5	6-8	0-16	
Optional Troops										
Javelinmen	Light Foot	Unprotected	Average	Undrilled	Javelins	Light Spear	4	6-8	0-16	
Allies										
Galwegian allies										
Strathclyde allies (Only before 945) – Post-Roman British										
Viking allies										

EARLY SCOTS ALLIES

Allied commander	Field Commander/Troop Commander						40/25	1	
Troop name	Troop Type				Capabilities		Points per base	Bases per BG	Total bases
	Type	Armour	Quality	Training	Shooting	Close Combat			
Cavalry	Cavalry	Protected	Average	Undrilled	-	Light Spear, Swordsmen	9	4	0-4
	Light Horse	Unprotected	Average	Undrilled	Javelins	Light Spear	7	4	
Thegns	Heavy Foot	Armoured	Superior	Undrilled	-	Impact Foot, Swordsmen	12	4	0-4
		Protected					9		
	Heavy Foot	Armoured	Superior	Undrilled	-	Offensive Spearmen	12	4	
		Protected					9		
Spearmen	Medium Foot	Protected	Average	Undrilled	-	Offensive spearmen	7	8-10	8-24
Archers	Light Foot	Unprotected	Average	Undrilled	Bow	-	5	4-6	0-6
Javelinmen	Light Foot	Unprotected	Average	Undrilled	Javelins	Light Spear	4	4-6	

GALWEGIAN ALLIES									
Allied commander	Field Commander/Troop Commander						40/25	1	
Troop name	Troop Type				Capabilities		Points per base	Bases per BG	Total bases
	Type	Armour	Quality	Training	Shooting	Close Combat			
Warriors	Medium Foot	Protected	Average	Undrilled	-	Impact Foot, Swordsmen	7	8-12	8-36
		Unprotected					6		

RUS

By the mid 9th century AD, Vikings (mainly of Swedish origin) had long been established as traders and raiders along the major rivers of Russia. In 860 they sailed across the Black Sea with 200 ships and raided Constantinople itself. About the same time, according to the earliest Russian chronicles, a Varangian (Viking) named Rurik was selected as ruler by several Slavic and Finno-Ugrian tribes in north-west Russia, first establishing himself at Novgorod. He later moved south and established control over Kiev (the capital of modern Ukraine), ending the tribute to the Khazar Khaganate. He was the founder of the Rurikid dynasty, who provided the princes that ruled Russia throughout the Middle Ages.

Rus Commander and Druzhina

Prince Oleg (Helgi), founded the so-called Kievan Rus circa 880. He expanded Rus control over the local tribes. In 911 a trade agreement was signed between the Rus and the Byzantine Empire. The Kievan state controlled the major trade routes from the Baltic and Germany to the Black Sea, the Khazar Khaganate and the East, and was rich in export goods such as furs, beeswax and honey.

By the reign of Svyatoslav I (945–972) Kievan princes had adopted Slavic names, but their druzhina (retained troops) were still mainly of Scandinavian origin. Around 968 Svyatoslav decisively defeated the Khazar Khaganate and sacked the Khazar capital Atil. Around the same time he also invaded the Bulgarian Empire and dealt it a series of defeats from which it would never recover.

Vladimir the Great (980–1015) adopted Orthodox Christianity. The peak of Kievan power came in his reign and that of Yaroslav the Wise (1019–1054). By then the Kievan state included modern Belarus, Ukraine and western Russia. Thereafter endemic internecine strife between the steadily increasing numbers of Rurikid princes broke the state up into numerous rival principalities.

This list covers Rus armies from 860 until the mid 11th century.

TROOP NOTES

The standard Rus battlefield formation was the shieldwall, comprising men armed with various combinations of sword, axe, throwing spears and thrusting spears. This formation is best represented under the rules as Offensive Spearmen.

Not much use was made of archery by the Rus themselves, archers being supplied by Slav or Turkic auxiliaries. Foot archers were massed on the wings on the final day of the Battle of Dorostolon against the Byzantines. They must have been somewhere else earlier in the battle, so we allow them the option to be included as supporting LF in spearmen battle groups.

Druzhina usually fought on foot, but sometimes fought mounted.

RUS STARTER ARMY		
Commander-in-Chief	1	Field Commander
Sub-commanders	2	2 x Troop Commander
Druzhina	1 BG	6 bases of druzhina: Average, Armoured, Undrilled Cavalry – Light Spear, Swordsmen
Spearmen	5 BGs	Each comprising 8 bases of spearmen: Average, Protected, Undrilled Heavy Foot – Offensive Spearmen
Archers	1 BG	8 bases of archers: Average, Unprotected, Undrilled Light Foot – Bow
Mercenary horse archers	2 BGs	Each comprising 4 bases of mercenary horse archers: Average, Unprotected, Undrilled Light Horse – Bow, Swordsmen
Camp	1	Unfortified camp
Total	9 BGs	Camp, 14 mounted bases, 48 foot bases, 3 commanders

BUILDING A CUSTOMISED LIST USING OUR ARMY POINTS

Choose an army based on the maxima and minima in the list below. The following special instructions apply to this army:

- Commanders should be depicted as druzhina.
- Druzhina can always dismount as Heavy Foot, Armoured, Superior, Undrilled, Offensive Spearmen.
- Rus allied commanders' contingents must conform to the Rus allies list below, but the troops in the contingent are deducted from the minima and maxima in the main list.
- Apart from Pechenegs with Poles, only one non-Rus ally can be used.

Kievan commanders, by Angus McBride. Taken from Men-at-Arms 333: Armies of Medieval Russia 750–1250.

RUS									
Territory Types: Agricultural, Steppes, Woodlands									
C-in-C	Inspired Commander/Field Commander/Troop Commander						80/50/35	1	
Sub-commanders	Field Commander						50	0-2	
	Troop Commander						35	0-3	
Rus allied commanders	Field Commander/Troop Commander						40/25	0-2	
Troop name	Troop Type				Capabilities		Points per base	Bases per BG	Total bases
	Type	Armour	Quality	Training	Shooting	Close Combat			
Core Troops									
Druzhina	Heavy Foot	Armoured	Superior	Undrilled	-	Offensive Spearmen	12	6-8	0-8
	Cavalry	Armoured	Average	Undrilled	-	Light Spear, Swordsmen	12	4-6	
Spearmen	Heavy Foot	Protected	Average	Undrilled	-	Offensive Spearmen	7	6-8	32-128
Optional Troops									
Foot archers attached to spearmen battle groups to form 1/3 of battle group	Light Foot	Unprotected	Average	Drilled	Bow	-	5	3 (1/3 of 9)	0-16
Separately deployed foot archers	Light Foot	Unprotected	Average	Undrilled	Bow	-	5	6-8	
	Medium Foot	Unprotected	Average	Undrilled	Bow	-	5		
Alan, Bulgar, Magyar, Pecheneg or Oghuz mercenaries — Only from 960	Light Horse	Unprotected	Average	Undrilled	Bow	Swordsmen	10	4-6	0-12
	Cavalry	Unprotected	Average	Undrilled	Bow	Swordsmen	10		
		Protected					11		
Fortified Camp							24		0-1
Allies									
Bulgar allies (Only from 968 to 971) – Early Bulgar – See Field of Glory Companion 7: *Decline and Fall: Byzantium at War*									
Pecheneg allies (Only from 968) – See Field of Glory Companion 7: *Decline and Fall: Byzantium at War*									
Viking allies									
Special Campaigns									
Only Sviatopolk the Accursed in 1018									
Polish allies (Only in 1018) – Early Polish									
Pecheneg allies must also be used									

RUS ALLIES									
Allied commander	Field Commander/Troop Commander						40/25	1	
Troop name	Troop Type				Capabilities		Points per base	Bases per BG	Total bases
	Type	Armour	Quality	Training	Shooting	Close Combat			
Druzhina	Heavy Foot	Armoured	Superior	Undrilled	-	Offensive Spearmen	12	4	0-4
	Cavalry	Armoured	Average	Undrilled	-	Light Spear, Swordsmen	12	4	
Spearmen	Heavy Foot	Protected	Average	Undrilled	-	Offensive Spearmen	7	6-8	8-32

NORSE-IRISH

The first recorded Viking raid on Ireland was in 795 AD when Norwegian Vikings looted the island of Rathlin off the North coast. Early raids were mostly small-scale, but from the 840s the Vikings were wintering in Ireland and establishing permanent settlements. These included Dublin, Limerick, Waterford, Wexford, Cork and Arklow. They used these as bases from which to raid inland. In between fighting among themselves, the native Irish kingdoms resisted the Vikings. Eventually the Viking (Ostmen) settlements became part of the confused political scene in Ireland, with alliances between Irish and Vikings against other Vikings and/or Irish commonplace. The Leinstermen, for example, were usually allied to the Dublin or Limerick Vikings. In the course of this interaction, Irish warriors came to adopt the Viking axe as their favourite weapon.

At Clontarf in 1014, the Irish army under High King Brian Boru defeated a combined army of Leinster Irish under King Maelmordha and Vikings under Jarls Brodir of Man and Sigurd of Orkney. The Irish army also included a small force of Manx Vikings. Following this defeat, Viking power in Ireland declined.

This list covers native Irish armies from the late 9th century when the Irish began to adopt Viking style weapons until the first Anglo-Norman mercenaries were imported in 1167. Soon after, the Norman conquest of Ireland began.

Norse Irish Commander

TROOP NOTES

Irish warriors of this period were armed with short thrusting spear, javelins and big axes. Although Giraldus Cambrensis describes the Irish axe as used in one hand, several contemporary illustrations, including in his own manuscript, show it being used two-handed. Giraldus states that neither helmet nor mail were any protection against it. "The whole thigh of a soldier, though ever so well cased in iron mail, is cut off by one blow of the axe, the thigh and the leg falling on one side of the horse, and the dying body on the

Norse-Irish Jarl (mounted) *and Anglo-Danish mercenaries, by Angus McBride.* Taken from *Men-at-Arms* 154: Arthur and the Anglo-Saxon Wars.

other". We therefore allow players the option to treat all such axes as heavy weapon, or only those used two-handed. In the latter case, battle groups graded as light spear, swordsmen are those with a low proportion of men using two-handed axes.

Armour was rare amongst Irish troops and shields were uncommon.

Skirmishes and ambushes were favoured, but Irish foot sometimes formed up in close order for pitched battle, as at Clontarf .

Norse-Irish Levy

Although wealthier men often rode to battle, they fought on foot. The first account of massed mounted combat was in 1131, when the *marcshluag* ("steed-host") of Munster defeated that of Connacht.

Bands of landless adventurers hired themselves out as mercenaries. They were variously known in this period as *Meic Mallachtain* (Sons of Malediction), *Macca Bais* (Sons of Death) or *Gall-Gaedhil* (Foreign Irish). Some modelled themselves on the former pagan *Diberga* and *Fianna* warrior cults, who shaved their hair at the front and grew it long and plaited at the back.

NORSE IRISH STARTER ARMY		
Commander-in-Chief	1	Inspired Commander (Brian Boru)
Sub-commanders	2	2 x Troop Commander
Nobles and retainers	2 BGs	Each comprising 8 bases of nobles and retainers: Superior, Unprotected, Undrilled Heavy Foot – Heavy Weapon
Other warriors	5 BGs	Each comprising 8 bases of other warriors: Average, Unprotected, Undrilled Medium Foot – Heavy Weapon
Other warriors	4 BGs	Each comprising 6 bases of other warriors: Average, Unprotected, Undrilled Light Foot – Javelins, Light Spear
Camp	1	Unfortified camp
Total	11 BGs	Camp, 80 foot bases, 3 commanders

BUILDING A CUSTOMISED LIST USING OUR ARMY POINTS

Choose an army based on the maxima and minima in the list below. The following special instructions apply to this army:

- Commanders should be depicted as nobles and retainers.
- Irish allied commanders' contingents must conform to the Norse-Irish allies list below, but the troops in the contingent are deducted from the minima and maxima in the main list.
- Nobles and retainers upgraded to cavalry can always dismount as Medium Foot, Unprotected, Superior, Undrilled, Heavy Weapon.

NORSE-IRISH										
Territory Types: Agricultural, Hilly, Woodlands										
C-in-C		Inspired Commander/Field Commander/Troop Commander						80/50/35	1	
Sub-commanders		Field Commander/Troop Commander						50/35	0-2	
Irish allied commanders		Field Commander/Troop Commander						40/25	0-2	
Troop name		Troop Type				Capabilities		Points per base	Bases per BG	Total bases
		Type	Armour	Quality	Training	Shooting	Close Combat			
Core Troops										
Nobles and retainers		Medium or Heavy Foot	Unprotected	Superior	Undrilled	-	Heavy Weapon	7	6-8	6-16
Other warriors		Medium Foot	Unprotected	Average	Undrilled	-	Heavy Weapon	6	6-8	24-120
		Medium Foot	Unprotected	Average	Undrilled	-	Light Spear, Swordsmen	5	6-8	
		Light Foot	Unprotected	Average	Undrilled	Javelins	Light Spear	4	6-8	6-40
Optional Troops										
Upgrade nobles and retainers to cavalry	Only from 1131	Cavalry	Protected	Average	Undrilled	-	Light Spear, Swordsmen	9	4-6	Any
Meic Mallachtain etc.		Medium Foot	Unprotected	Superior	Undrilled	-	Heavy Weapon	7	6-8	0-8
Levies		Light Foot	Unprotected	Poor	Undrilled	Javelins	Light Spear	2	6-8	0-36
Slingers		Light Foot	Unprotected	Average	Undrilled	Sling	-	4	4-6	0-6
Archers		Light Foot	Unprotected	Average	Undrilled	Bow	-	5	4-6	
Trenches, abatis or plashing		Field Fortifications						3		0-24
Fortified Camp								24		0-1
Allies										
Viking or Ostmen Allies – Viking										

NORSE-IRISH ALLIES									
Allied commander	Field Commander/Troop Commander						40/25	1	
Troop name	Troop Type				Capabilities		Points per base	Bases per BG	Total bases
	Type	Armour	Quality	Training	Shooting	Close Combat			
Nobles and retainers	Medium or Heavy Foot	Unprotected	Superior	Undrilled	-	Heavy Weapon	7	4-6	0-6
Other warriors	Medium Foot	Unprotected	Average	Undrilled	-	Heavy Weapon	6	6-8	6-32
	Medium Foot	Unprotected	Average	Undrilled	-	Light Spear, Swordsmen	5	6-8	
	Light Foot	Unprotected	Average	Undrilled	Javelins	Light Spear	4	6-8	0-12
Levies	Light Foot	Unprotected	Poor	Undrilled	Javelins	Light Spear	2	6-8	0-12

EARLY MEDIEVAL FRENCH

Although Count Odo of Paris was elected King of West Francia in 888 following the death of Charles the Fat, by 898 the throne was once again in the hands of a Carolingian, Charles III. In 911 he granted the lower Seine area, henceforth known as Normandy, to the Viking leader Rollo (Rolf). In 922 Odo's brother Robert revolted and was crowned king as Robert I. He defeated Charles at Soissons in 923 but was himself killed in the battle. Rudolph, Duke of Burgundy, was then elected King. Charles died in prison in 929.

On Rudolph's death in 936, Charles' son Louis IV was recalled from exile in England and crowned king. He reigned till 954 when he died after falling from his horse. His son Lothair fought wars in Flanders and Germany and even captured the Emperor Otto II's capital in 978, adding to the insult by reversing the direction of the eagle on top of the palace. Otto then counterattacked into France, reaching Paris but failing to take it. Peace was concluded in 980. Lothair died in 986, and was succeeded by his son Louis V the Indolent, the last Carolingian King of West Francia, who died young in 987.

Following his death, Hugh Capet, Duke of France, descendant of King Robert I and the dominant force in the kingdom for the preceding decade, was elected King. He was the founder of the Capetian dynasty who ruled France until 1328 in the main line, and in collateral lines until the end of the French monarchy. His actual power, however, extended only over a small part of France around Paris and Orleans, the rest being under the control of the great nobles. This weakness was a characteristic of the French monarchy in the early Capetian period, to the extent that in the late 12th century the Angevin Kings of England ruled more territory in France than the King of France himself.

On Hugh's death in 996, his son Robert II succeeded to the throne. In an attempt to increase his power, he tried to annexe any feudal lands whose title became vacant, which usually resulted in war with a rival claimant. He did succeed in acquiring the Duchy of Burgundy by 1016. He died in 1031, in the middle of a civil war against his sons.

During the reign of Robert's son Henry I (1031–1060), the royal demesne shrank to its lowest ebb, Burgundy being alienated again to placate his brother Robert.

This list covers the armies of the Kingdom of West Francia (France) from 888 until 1050.

TROOP NOTES

Cavalry battle groups are treated as Armoured or Protected depending on the proportion of men with mail coats. As time went on, the proportion with mail increased.

Crossbowman

French Commander

French miles and levy, by Angus McBride. Taken from Men-at-Arms 231: French Medieval Armies 1000–1300.

EARLY MEDIEVAL FRENCH STARTER ARMY		
Commander-in Chief	1	Field Commander
Sub-commanders	2	2 x Troop Commander
Frankish cavalry	5 BGs	Each comprising 4 bases of Frankish cavalry: Superior, Armoured, Undrilled Cavalry – Lancers, Swordsmen
Spearmen	2 BGs	Each comprising 8 bases of Spearmen: Average, Protected, Undrilled Heavy Foot – Defensive Spearmen
Archers	2 BGs	Each comprising 6 bases of archers: Average, Unprotected, Undrilled Light Foot – Bow
Camp	1	Unfortified camp
Total	9 BGs	Camp, 20 mounted bases, 28 foot bases, 3 commanders

BUILDING A CUSTOMISED LIST USING OUR ARMY POINTS

Choose an army based on the maxima and minima in the list below. The following special instructions apply to this army:

- Commanders should be depicted as cavalry.
- French allied commanders' contingents must conform to the Early Medieval French allies list below, but the troops in the contingent are deducted from the minima and maxima in the main list.

Spearman

EARLY MEDIEVAL FRENCH

Territory Types: Agricultural, Woodlands

C-in-C		Inspired Commander/Field Commander/Troop Commander						80/50/35	1	
Sub-commanders		Field Commander						50	0-2	
		Troop Commander						35	0-3	
French allied commanders		Field Commander/Troop Commander						40/25	0-2	
Troop name		Troop Type				Capabilities		Points per base	Bases per BG	Total bases
		Type	Armour	Quality	Training	Shooting	Close Combat			
Core Troops										
Frankish cavalry		Cavalry	Armoured	Superior	Undrilled	-	Lancers, Swordsmen	16	4-6	12-54
			Protected					12		
Spearmen		Heavy Foot	Protected	Average	Undrilled	-	Defensive Spearmen	6	6-8	0-24
Optional Troops										
Foot archers		Light Foot	Unprotected	Average	Undrilled	Bow	-	5	6-8	0-12
		Medium Foot	Unprotected	Average	Undrilled	Bow	-	5	6-8	
Crossbowmen	Any date	Light Foot	Unprotected	Average	Undrilled	Crossbow	-	5	4-6	0-6
	Only from 950	Medium Foot	Protected	Average	Undrilled	Crossbow	-	6	4-6	
Gascon javelinmen		Light Foot	Unprotected	Average	Undrilled	Javelins	Light Spear	4	4-6	0-6
Gascon cavalry		Light Horse	Unprotected	Average	Undrilled	Javelins	Light Spear	7	4	0-4
Peasants		Mob	Unprotected	Poor	Undrilled	-	-	2	8-12	0-12
Allies										
Viking allies (Only before 923)										
Norman allies (Only from 923)										

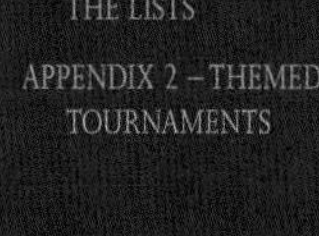

EARLY MEDIEVAL FRENCH ALLIES

Allied commander	Field Commander/Troop Commander						40/25	1	
Troop name	Troop Type				Capabilities		Points per base	Bases per BG	Total bases
	Type	Armour	Quality	Training	Shooting	Close Combat			
Frankish cavalry	Cavalry	Armoured	Superior	Undrilled	-	Lancers, Swordsmen	16	4-6	4-16
		Protected					12		
Spearmen	Heavy Foot	Protected	Average	Undrilled	-	Defensive Spearmen	6	6-8	0-8
Foot archers	Light Foot	Unprotected	Average	Undrilled	Bow	-	5	4	0-4
	Medium Foot	Unprotected	Average	Undrilled	Bow	-	5	4	

EARLY MEDIEVAL GERMAN

Following the death of Charles the Fat in 888, the Frankish Empire was permanently divided. East Francia (Germany) fell to Arnulf of Carinthia, an illegitimate son of the late Carolingian King Carloman of Bavaria. On his death in 899, he was succeeded by his six year old son, Louis the Child. During Louis' reign East Francia was ravaged by the Magyars, German armies suffering defeats at Pressburg in 907 and Augsburg in 910. Louis died in 911, at the age of eighteen, the last Carolingian King of East Francia.

Following his death, Conrad I, Duke of Franconia was elected King of East Francia. Following his death at the end of 918, Henry I the Fowler, Duke of Saxony, was elected King. After a defeat in 924, he won a victory over the Magyars at Riade in 933. On his death in 936, he was succeeded by his son Otto I the Great. After suppressing the rebellious dukes of Germany, Otto invaded Italy in 951 and established control over the Kingdom of Italy. In 955 he decisively defeated the Magyars at Lechfeld and the West Slavic Obodrite confederation at Recknitz.

As a matter of policy, Otto strengthened the ecclesiastical authorities in Germany, subject to the monarchy, at the expense of the secular nobility. In 962 he was crowned Holy Roman Emperor by Pope John XII. In 972 this title was recognised by the Byzantine Emperor John I Tzimiskes. Otto died in 973, succeeded by his son Otto II. The Saxon (Ottonian) dynasty lasted until the death of Henry II in 1024. Thereafter Conrad II was elected King and Emperor, the founder of the Salian dynasty that ruled Germany until 1125.

This list covers armies of the Kingdom of East Francia (Germany) from 888 until 1050.

German Spearman

TROOP NOTES

Cavalry from some parts of Germany, notably Swabians, Old Saxons and Thuringians, often fought on foot.

Cavalry battle groups are treated as Armoured or Protected depending on the proportion of men with mail coats.

German Cavalry

EARLY MEDIEVAL GERMAN STARTER ARMY		
Commander-in-Chief	1	Field Commander
Sub-commanders	2	2 x Troop Commander
Cavalry	3 BGs	Each comprising 4 bases of cavalry: Superior, Armoured, Undrilled Cavalry – Lancers, Swordsmen
Thuringian cavalry	2 BGs	Each comprising 4 bases of Thuringian cavalry: Average, Armoured, Undrilled Cavalry – Light Spear, Swordsmen
Spearmen	3 BGs	Each comprising 8 bases of Spearmen: Average, Protected, Undrilled Heavy Foot – Defensive Spearmen
Archers	1 BG	8 bases of archers: Average, Unprotected, Undrilled Light Foot – Bow
Camp	1	Unfortified camp
Total	9 BGs	Camp, 20 mounted bases, 32 foot bases, 3 commanders

BUILDING A CUSTOMISED LIST USING OUR ARMY POINTS

Choose an army based on the maxima and minima in the list below. The following special instructions apply to this army:

- Commanders should be depicted as cavalry.
- Cavalry can always dismount as Heavy Foot, Armoured or Protected (as mounted type), Superior, Undrilled, Offensive Spearmen.
- The minimum marked * applies if any foot are used.
- German allied commanders' contingents must conform to the Early Medieval German allies list below, but the troops in the contingent are deducted from the minima and maxima in the main list.
- Magyar, Polish or Slav allies cannot be used with Burgundians or Lombards.

EARLY MEDIEVAL GERMAN										
Territory Types: Agricultural, Hilly, Woodlands										
C-in-C		Inspired Commander/Field Commander/Troop Commander						80/50/35	1	
Sub-commanders		Field Commander						50	0-2	
		Troop Commander						35	0-3	
German allied commanders		Field Commander/Troop Commander						40/25	0-2	
Troop name		Troop Type				Capabilities		Points per base	Bases per BG	Total bases
		Type	Armour	Quality	Training	Shooting	Close Combat			
Core Troops										
Cavalry		Cavalry	Armoured	Superior	Undrilled	-	Lancers, Swordsmen	16	4-6	8-48
			Armoured	Average				12		
			Protected	Superior				12		
			Protected	Average				9		
Spearmen	Before 933	Heavy Foot	Protected	Average	Undrilled	-	Defensive Spearmen	6	6-8	16-72
	From 933									*8-36
Optional Troops										
Old Saxon, Slav or Thuringian cavalry		Cavalry	Armoured	Average	Undrilled	-	Light Spear, Swordsmen	12	4-6	0-8
			Protected					9		
Foot archers		Light Foot	Unprotected	Average	Undrilled	Bow	-	5	6-8	0-12
		Medium Foot	Unprotected	Average	Undrilled	Bow	-	5	6-8	
Peasants		Mob	Unprotected	Poor	Undrilled	-	-	2	8-12	0-12
Allies										
Burgundian allies (Only from 933) – Early Medieval French										
Lombard allies										
Magyar allies (Only from 892 to 894)										
Polish allies (Only from 1045) – Early Polish										
Slav allies – Great Moravian										

EARLY MEDIEVAL GERMAN ALLIES									
Allied commander	Field Commander/Troop Commander						40/25	1	
Troop name	Troop Type				Capabilities		Points per base	Bases per BG	Total bases
	Type	Armour	Quality	Training	Shooting	Close Combat			
Cavalry	Cavalry	Armoured	Superior	Undrilled	-	Lancers, Swordsmen	16	4-6	4-16
		Armoured	Average				12		
		Protected	Superior				12		
		Protected	Average				9		
Spearmen	Heavy Foot	Protected	Average	Undrilled	-	Defensive Spearmen	6	6-8	0-12
Foot archers	Light Foot	Unprotected	Average	Undrilled	Bow	-	5	4	0-4
	Medium Foot	Unprotected	Average	Undrilled	Bow	-	5	4	

NORMAN

Normandy (in northern France) was created by the treaty of Saint-Clair-sur-Epte in 911 AD by which the King of France granted lands around the lower Seine to Rollo (Rolf), leader of the Vikings who had settled there. Following this the Normans rapidly assimilated to the French language and military system, to which they added their native Viking fierceness. Over the course of the 10th century the County of Normandy expanded at the expense of its neighbours. The ducal title became established circa 1000, the first Duke being Richard II.

In 1066 Duke William the Bastard invaded England where he defeated and killed King Harold at the Battle of Hastings. He was subsequently crowned King of England, though he also remained Duke of Normandy owing (increasingly theoretical) fealty to the King of France.

Miles

Norman adventurers hired themselves out as mercenaries in Italy and in the Byzantine Empire. Those in southern Italy, under the leadership of the de Hauteville family, carved out a kingdom for themselves in the mid-11th century. Roussel de Bailleul, a Norman mercenary in Byzantine service, rebelled and carved out an independent state in Asia Minor in the 1070s following the Byzantine defeat by the Seljuk Turks at Manzikert. Unlike the Italo-Norman kingdom, his princedom proved short-lived and he was eventually executed for his treachery.

This list covers the armies of the County (later Duchy) of Normandy from 923 until the effective end of English resistance to the Norman conquest in 1071. The Normans in Italy are covered by their own list in a subsequent volume.

TROOP NOTES

The switch over from classifying *milites* as Cavalry to classifying them as Knights is arbitrary. However, the Norman charge was noted as particularly fierce at the Battle of Monte Maggiore against the Byzantines in 1041.

Norman bishop and troops, by *Angus McBride*. Taken from *Elite 9*: The Normans.

NORMAN STARTER ARMY (1066 AD)		
Commander-in-Chief	1	Inspired Commander (Duke William)
Sub-commanders	2	2 x Troop Commander
Milites	3 BGs	Each comprising 4 bases of milites: Superior, Armoured, Undrilled Knights – Lancers, Swordsmen
Milites lacking horses	1 BG	6 bases of milites: Superior, Armoured, Undrilled Heavy Foot – Offensive Spearmen
Spearmen	2 BGs	Each comprising 6 bases of Spearmen: Average, Protected, Undrilled Heavy Foot – Defensive Spearmen
Archers	2 BGs	Each comprising 6 bases of archers: Average, Unprotected, Undrilled Light Foot – Bow
Camp	1	Unfortified camp
Total	8 BGs	Camp, 12 mounted bases, 30 foot bases, 3 commanders

BUILDING A CUSTOMISED LIST USING OUR ARMY POINTS

Choose an army based on the maxima and minima in the list below. The following special instructions apply to this army:

- Commanders should be depicted as *milites*.
- *Milites* can always dismount as Heavy Foot, Armoured, Superior, Undrilled, Offensive Spearmen.

Dismouted Miles

Hastings, 14 October 1066, by Angus McBride. Taken from Elite 9: The Normans.

NORMAN										
Territory Types: Agricultural, Woodlands										
C-in-C		Inspired Commander/Field Commander/Troop Commander						80/50/35	1	
Sub-commanders		Field Commander						50	0-2	
		Troop Commander						35	0-3	
Troop name		**Troop Type**				**Capabilities**		**Points per base**	**Bases per BG**	**Total bases**
		Type	Armour	Quality	Training	Shooting	Close Combat			
Core Troops										
Milites	Before 1041	Cavalry	Armoured	Superior	Undrilled	-	Lancers, Swordsmen	16	4-6	12-56
	From 1041	Knights	Armoured	Superior	Undrilled	-	Lancers, Swordsmen	20		
Spearmen		Heavy Foot	Protected	Average	Undrilled	-	Defensive Spearmen	6	6-8	0-24
Optional Troops										
Foot archers		Light Foot	Unprotected	Average	Undrilled	Bow	-	5	6-8	0-12
		Medium Foot	Unprotected	Average	Undrilled	Bow	-	5	6-8	
Crossbowmen	Any date	Light Foot	Unprotected	Average	Undrilled	Crossbow	-	5	4-6	0-6
	Only from 950	Medium Foot	Protected	Average	Undrilled	Crossbow	-	6	4-6	
Peasants		Mob	Unprotected	Poor	Undrilled	-	-	2	8-12	0-12
Allies										
French allies – Early Medieval French (Before 1051) or Feudal French (From 1051) – See Field of Glory Companion 10: *Oath of Fealty: Feudal Europe at War*										
Special Campaigns										
Only Duke William's Invasion of England in 1066										
Downgrade milites lacking horses to:		Heavy Foot	Armoured	Superior	Undrilled	-	Offensive Spearmen	12	6-8	1/3 – 2/3

NORMAN ALLIES										
Allied commander		Field Commander/Troop Commander						40/25	1	
Troop name		**Troop Type**				**Capabilities**		**Points per base**	**Bases per BG**	**Total bases**
		Type	Armour	Quality	Training	Shooting	Close Combat			
Milites	Before 1041	Cavalry	Armoured	Superior	Undrilled	-	Lancers, Swordsmen	16	4-6	4-16
	From 1041	Knights	Armoured	Superior	Undrilled	-	Lancers, Swordsmen	20		
Spearmen		Heavy Foot	Protected	Average	Undrilled	-	Defensive Spearmen	6	6-8	0-8
Foot archers		Light Foot	Unprotected	Average	Undrilled	Bow	-	5	4	0-4
		Medium Foot	Unprotected	Average	Undrilled	Bow	-	5	4	

EARLY POLISH

In 966 AD Mieszko I, leader of the Slavic tribe of Polans, accepted Christianity. This marked the creation of the Polish state and the foundation of the Piast dynasty. By the end of his reign he had transformed Poland into one of the strongest states in Eastern Europe. His son Bolesław the Brave continued his work and became the first King of Poland in 1025. A period of instability under Boleslaw's son, Mieszko II, was followed by a resurgence under his son, Casimir the Restorer, who reigned till 1058.

This list covers Polish armies from 966 until 1058.

TROOP NOTES

Polish cavalry in this period often relied on hit and run tactics, including feigned flight.

The wealthier infantrymen formed up as heavy spearmen, in leather or padded linen sleeveless armour, sometimes reinforced with leather strips or small iron plates, and with a substantial shield.

Peasant foot, sometimes equipped only with clubs, nevertheless also often carried shields.

Ambushes and skirmishes were preferred, but when pitched battle was unavoidable, the Poles usually formed up with two lines of cavalry in the centre, spearmen on each side of them and peasant archers angled forwards on the wings.

Peasant Archer

Polish Spearmen

EARLY POLISH STARTER ARMY		
Commander-in-Chief	1	Field Commander
Sub-commanders	2	2 x Troop Commander
Noble cavalry	4 BGs	Each comprising 4 bases of noble cavalry: Superior, Armoured, Undrilled Cavalry – Light Spear, Swordsmen
Spearmen	2 BGs	Each comprising 8 bases of spearmen: Average, Protected, Undrilled Heavy Foot – Defensive Spearmen
Peasant archers	2 BGs	Each comprising 8 bases of peasant archers: Average, Protected, Undrilled Medium Foot – Bow
Peasant slingers	1 BG	8 bases of peasant slingers: Average, Unprotected, Undrilled Light Foot – Sling
Camp	1	Unfortified camp
Total	9 BGs	Camp, 16 mounted bases, 40 foot bases, 3 commanders

BUILDING A CUSTOMISED LIST USING OUR ARMY POINTS

Choose an army based on the maxima and minima in the list below. The following special instructions apply to this army:

- Commanders should be depicted as noble cavalry.
- Polish allied commanders' contingents must conform to the Early Polish allies list below, but the troops in the contingent are deducted from the minima and maxima in the main list.
- Only one foreign allied contingent can be used.

EARLY POLISH									
Territory Types: Agricultural, Woodlands									
C-in-C	Inspired Commander/Field Commander/Troop Commander						80/50/35	1	
Sub-commanders	Field Commander						50	0-2	
	Troop Commander						35	0-3	
Polish allied commanders	Field Commander/Troop Commander						40/25	0-2	
Troop name	Troop Type				Capabilities		Points per base	Bases per BG	Total bases
	Type	Armour	Quality	Training	Shooting	Close Combat			
Core Troops									
Noble cavalry	Cavalry	Armoured	Superior	Undrilled	-	Light Spear, Swordsmen	16	4-6	6-28
Spearmen	Heavy Foot	Protected	Average	Undrilled	-	Defensive Spearmen	6	6-8	12-48
Peasant archers	Light Foot	Unprotected	Average	Undrilled	Bow	-	5	6-8	12-56
	Medium Foot	Unprotected	Average	Undrilled	Bow	-	5	6-8	
	Medium Foot	Protected	Average	Undrilled	Bow	-	6	6-8	
Optional Troops									
Peasant slingers	Light Foot	Unprotected	Average	Undrilled	Sling	-	4	6-8	0-12
Poorly equipped peasants	Mob	Unprotected	Poor	Undrilled	-	-	2	8-12	0-20
		Protected					3		
Allies									
Rus Allies									
Viking allies									

Polish heavy cavalryman, by Graham Turner. Taken from Men-at-Arms 310:
German Medieval Armies 1000–1300.

EARLY POLISH ALLIES									
Allied commander	Field Commander/Troop Commander						40/25	1	
Troop name	Troop Type				Capabilities		Points per base	Bases per BG	Total bases
	Type	Armour	Quality	Training	Shooting	Close Combat			
Noble cavalry	Cavalry	Armoured	Superior	Undrilled	-	Light Spear, Swordsmen	16	4-6	4-8
Spearmen	Heavy Foot	Protected	Average	Undrilled	-	Defensive Spearmen	6	6-8	6-16
Peasant archers	Light Foot	Unprotected	Average	Undrilled	Bow	-	5	6-8	6-18
	Medium Foot	Unprotected	Average	Undrilled	Bow	-	5	6-8	
	Medium Foot	Protected	Average	Undrilled	Bow	-	6	6-8	

ANGLO-DANISH

In 1013 King Sweyn Forkbeard of Denmark invaded England. The English King, Æthelred the Unready, fled to Normandy and Sweyn was accepted as King of England by the Witan and crowned on Christmas Day. In February of 1014, however, he died. His army elected his younger son Canute (Knut) as King of England, but then withdrew to Denmark. King Æthelred returned to England and was restored to the throne. In 1015, Canute reinvaded and by the end of 1016 was in control of the whole of England. Following his brother Harald's death in 1018, he was also King of Denmark.

On Cnut's death in 1035, Denmark fell to his son Hardicanute (Hardeknud), while England was ruled by his illegitimate half-brother Harold Harefoot, initially as regent for Hardicanute and later as king. Hardicanute was preparing to invade in 1040 to assert his right to the throne of England, but Harold conveniently died. When Hardicanute arrived he had his body exhumed, beheaded and thrown into a fen.

In 1042, Hardicanute died, having already recognised his English half-brother, Edward the Confessor, as his heir. Edward was the son of Æthelred the Unready by his second wife Emma of Normandy, who married Canute after Æthelred's death. Thus the English royal line of Wessex was restored to the throne.

Edward's reign was relatively peaceful, but when he died in January 1066 he had no generally accepted heir. Duke William of Normandy claimed to be his promised heir, but the Witan elected Harold Godwinson, Earl of Wessex, as King. King Harald Hardrada of Norway also claimed the throne on the basis of a supposed prior agreement between King Magnus of Norway and Hardicanute. Thus in 1066 England suffered two full scale invasions by the rival claimants to the throne.

King Harald landed in September, defeated the local fyrd at Fulford, near York, but was then defeated and killed by King Harold at Stamford Bridge just outside York. Duke William also landed in September, at Pevensey in Sussex. King Harold rushed south to meet him, but was defeated and killed near Hastings on October 14th. English resistance continued until 1071.

This list covers English armies from 1016 until 1071.

King Harold

TROOP NOTES

The standard Anglo-Saxon battle formation was the shieldwall (*bord-weal* or *scyld-burh*) much as described under the Viking list, though less use was made of archery.

The Huscarls were a permanently retained royal force of Danish mercenaries. They were

Select Fyrd

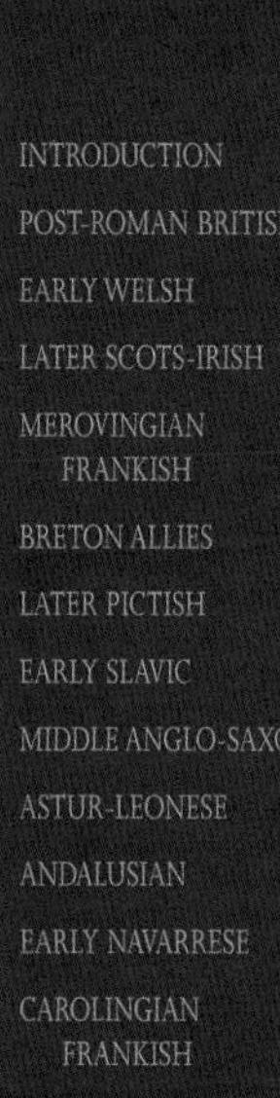

INTRODUCTION
POST-ROMAN BRITISH
EARLY WELSH
LATER SCOTS-IRISH
MEROVINGIAN FRANKISH
BRETON ALLIES
LATER PICTISH
EARLY SLAVIC
MIDDLE ANGLO-SAXON
ASTUR-LEONESE
ANDALUSIAN
EARLY NAVARRESE
CAROLINGIAN FRANKISH
LOMBARD ALLIES
VIKING
MAGYAR
GREAT MORAVIAN
EARLY SCOTS
RUS
NORSE-IRISH
EARLY MEDIEVAL FRENCH
EARLY MEDIEVAL GERMAN
NORMAN
EARLY POLISH
ANGLO-DANISH
APPENDIX 1 - USING THE LISTS
APPENDIX 2 – THEMED TOURNAMENTS

armed with two-handed axes, capable of felling a horse and rider with one blow. They normally wore iron mail, but were on at least one occasion deployed in leather armour with lighter weapons to fight the Welsh.

By this date the Select Fyrd, comprising thanes (minor noblemen) holding 5 or more hides of land, were expected to muster with sword, spear, shield, byrnie (mail coat), helmet and horse.

In emergencies the Great Fyrd would be summoned, consisting of all able-bodied freemen, but poorly trained and equipped. These would form up behind the Select Fyrd of their shire rather than in separate bodies. "Poor quality fyrd" represent such mixed bodies. We assume that even when the Great Fyrd was summoned, shires further from the site of the battle might supply only Select Fyrd, who could travel faster being mounted.

The conventional view is that huscarls and select fyrd nearly always fought on foot. Recent academic thinking, however, has challenged this "received wisdom", for which there is in fact little evidence. Although there are only a few accounts specifically stating that troops fought mounted, accounts stating that they fought on foot are also uncommon. Thus for most recorded battles we don't know whether troops fought on foot or mounted. There is, by contrast, much evidence for the importance of the horse in Anglo-Saxon warfare. Those interested in exploring the subject further are referred to Guy Halsall's *Warfare and Society in the Barbarian West*, 450-900, which, while not primarily covering the period of this list, discusses current thinking on Anglo-Saxon mounted combat. Evidence from the 11th century includes the Battle of Hereford (1055), where the entire English army fought on horseback, and also Snorri Sturluson's *Heimskringla*, which describes the English army fighting mounted at the Battle of Stamford Bridge (1066). Although Snorri's saga dates from the 13th century and has previously been discounted, large numbers of horseshoes have been found on the battlefield.

ANGLO-DANISH STARTER ARMY (1066 AD)		
Commander-in-Chief	1	Field Commander (King Harold)
Sub-commanders	2	2 x Troop Commander
Huscarls	2 BGs	Each comprising 6 bases of huscarls: Superior, Armoured, Undrilled Heavy Foot – Heavy Weapon
Select fyrd	2 BGs	Each comprising 8 bases of select fyrd: Average, Armoured, Undrilled Heavy Foot – Offensive Spearmen
Poor quality fyrd	4 BGs	Each comprising 8 bases of poor quality fyrd: Poor, Protected, Undrilled Heavy Foot – Offensive Spearmen
Slingers	1 BG	4 bases of slingers: Average, Unprotected, Undrilled Light Foot – Sling
Javelinmen	1 BG	4 bases of javelinmen: Average, Unprotected, Undrilled Light Foot – Javelins, Light Spear
Camp	1	Unfortified camp
Total	8 BGs	Camp, 68 foot bases, 3 commanders

Anglo-Danish troops, by Angus McBride. Taken from Men-at-Arms 154: Arthur and the Anglo-Saxon Wars.

BUILDING A CUSTOMISED LIST USING OUR ARMY POINTS

Choose an army based on the maxima and minima in the list below. The following special instructions apply to this army:

- Commanders should be depicted as huscarls.
- Huscarls listed as Cavalry can always dismount as Heavy Foot, Armoured, Superior, Undrilled, Heavy Weapon.
- Select fyrd listed as Cavalry can always dismount as Heavy Foot, Armoured, Average, Undrilled, Offensive Spearmen.
- Normans, lightened huscarls, Scots and Welsh cannot be used together.

ANGLO-DANISH										
Territory Types: Agricultural, Woodlands										
C-in-C		Inspired Commander/Field Commander/Troop Commander						80/50/35	1	
Sub-commanders		Field Commander						50	0-2	
		Troop Commander						35	0-3	
Troop name		Troop Type				Capabilities		Points per base	Bases per BG	Total bases
		Type	Armour	Quality	Training	Shooting	Close Combat			
Core Troops										
Huscarls		Heavy Foot	Armoured	Superior	Undrilled	-	Heavy Weapon	12	6-8	0-18
		Cavalry	Armoured	Superior	Undrilled	-	Light Spear, Swordsmen	16	4-6	
Select fyrd		Heavy Foot	Armoured	Average	Undrilled	-	Offensive Spearmen	9	6-8	16-40
Poor quality fyrd		Heavy Foot	Protected	Poor	Undrilled	-	Offensive Spearmen	5	8-10	0-96
		Mob	Unprotected	Poor	Undrilled	-	-	2	8-12	0-12
Optional Troops										
Normans	Only from 1042 to 1065	Knights	Armoured	Superior	Undrilled	-	Lancers, Swordsmen	20	4	0-4
Regrade huscarls in lightened equipment	Only from 1042 to 1065	Medium Foot	Protected	Superior	Undrilled		Light Spear, Swordsmen	8	6-8	All or none
Archers		Light Foot	Unprotected	Average	Undrilled	Bow	-	5	4-6	0-6
Slingers		Light Foot	Unprotected	Average	Undrilled	Sling	-	4	4-6	0-6
Javelinmen		Light Foot	Unprotected	Average	Undrilled	Javelins	Light Spear	4	4-6	0-6
Allies										
Scots exile allies (Only from 1042 to 1054) – Early Scots										
Viking allies										
Welsh allies										
Special Campaigns										
Only Earl Ralph the Timid in 1055										
Upgrade select fyrd to:		Cavalry	Armoured	Poor	Undrilled	-	Light Spear, Swordsmen	9	4-6	All
The following are not permitted: Inspired Commander, huscarls or any allies.										

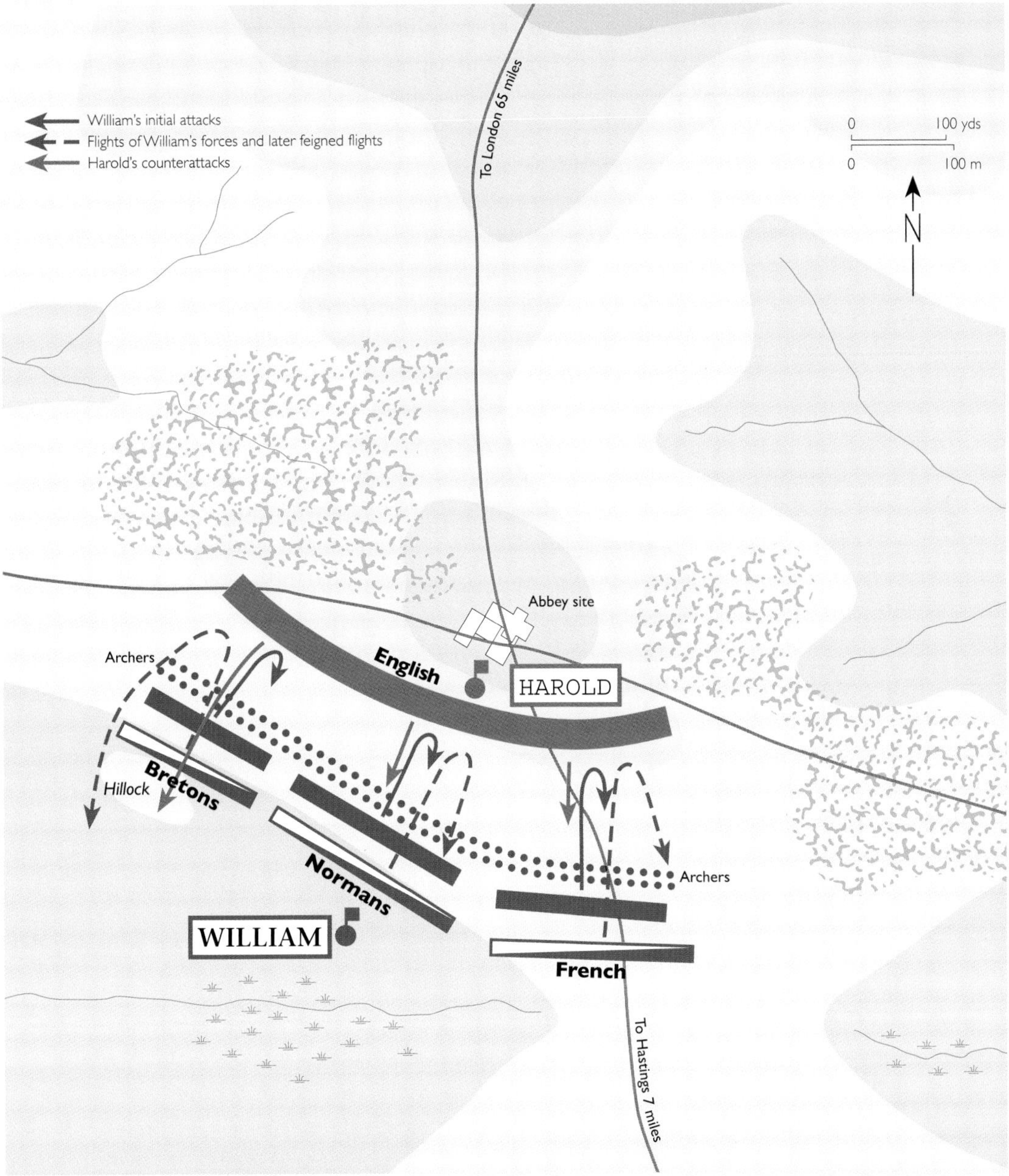

Hastings: dispositions, initial attacks and counterattacks. Taken from Essential Histories 12: Campaigns of the Norman Conquest.

ANGLO-DANISH ALLIES									
Allied commander	Field Commander/Troop Commander						40/25	1	
Troop name	**Troop Type**				**Capabilities**		**Points per base**	**Bases per BG**	**Total bases**
	Type	Armour	Quality	Training	Shooting	Close Combat			
Huscarls	Heavy Foot	Armoured	Superior	Undrilled	-	Heavy Weapon	12	4-6	0-6
	Cavalry	Armoured	Superior	Undrilled	-	Light Spear, Swordsmen	16	4-6	
Select fyrd	Heavy Foot	Armoured	Average	Undrilled	-	Offensive Spearmen	9	6-8	6-12
Poor quality fyrd	Heavy Foot	Protected	Poor	Undrilled	-	Offensive Spearmen	5	8-10	0-24

APPENDIX 1 – USING THE LISTS

To give balanced games, armies can be selected using the points system. The more effective the troops, the more each base costs in points. The maximum points for an army will usually be set at between 600 and 800 points for a singles game for 2 to 4 hours play. We recommend 800 points for 15mm singles tournament games (650 points for 25mm) and 1000 points for 15mm doubles games.

The army lists specify which troops can be used in a particular army. No other troops can be used. The number of bases of each type in the army must conform to the specified minima and maxima. Troops that have restrictions on when they can be used cannot be used with troops with a conflicting restriction. For example, troops that can only be used "before 600" cannot be used with troops that can only be used "from 600". All special instructions applying to an army list must be adhered to. They also apply to allied contingents supplied by the army.

Pictish Standard Bearer

All armies must have a C-in-C and at least one other commander. No army can have more than 4 commanders in total, including C-in-C, sub-commanders and allied commanders.

All armies must have a supply camp. This is free unless fortified. A fortified camp can only be used if specified in the army list. Field fortifications and portable defences can only be used if specified in the army list.

Allied contingents can only be used if specified in the army list. Most allied contingents have their own allied contingent list, to which they must conform unless the main army's list specifies otherwise.

BATTLE GROUPS

All troops are organized into battle groups. Commanders, supply camps and field fortifications are not troops and are not assigned to battle groups. Portable defences are not troops, but are assigned to specific battle groups.

Post Roman British *Army*

Battle groups must obey the following restrictions:

- The number of bases in a battle group must correspond to the range specified in the army list.
- Each battle group must initially comprise an even number of bases. The only exception to this rule is that battle groups whose army list specifies them as 2/3 of one type and 1/3 of another, can comprise 9 bases if this is within the battle group size range specified by the list.
- A battle group can only include troops from one line in a list, unless the list specifies a mixed formation by specifying fractions of the battle group to be of types from two lines. e.g. 2/3 spearmen, 1/3 archers.
- All troops in a battle group must be of the same quality and training. When a choice of quality or training is given in a list, this allows battle groups to differ from each other. It does not permit variety within a battle group.
- Unless specifically stated otherwise in an army list, all troops in a battle group must be of the same armour class. When a choice of armour class is given in a list, this allows battle groups to differ from each other. It does not permit variety within a battle group.

EXAMPLE LIST

Here is a section of an actual army list, which will help us to explain the basics and some special features. The list specifies the following items for each historical type included in the army:

- Troop Type - comprising Type, Armour, Quality and Training.
- Capabilities – comprising Shooting and Close Combat capabilities.
- Points cost per base.
- Minimum and maximum number of bases in each battle group.
- Minimum and maximum number of bases in the army.

<table>
<tr><th colspan="2" rowspan="2">Troop name</th><th colspan="4">Troop Type</th><th colspan="2">Capabilities</th><th rowspan="2">Points per base</th><th colspan="2" rowspan="2">Bases per BG</th><th colspan="2" rowspan="2">Total bases</th></tr>
<tr><th>Type</th><th>Armour</th><th>Quality</th><th>Training</th><th>Shooting</th><th>Close Combat</th></tr>
<tr><td rowspan="3">Noble cavalry</td><td>Any date</td><td>Cavalry</td><td>Armoured</td><td>Superior</td><td>Undrilled</td><td>-</td><td>Lancers, Swordsmen</td><td>16</td><td colspan="2">4-6</td><td>8-32</td><td rowspan="3">8-32</td></tr>
<tr><td rowspan="2">Only before 900</td><td rowspan="2">Cavalry</td><td rowspan="2">Protected</td><td>Superior</td><td rowspan="2">Undrilled</td><td rowspan="2">-</td><td rowspan="2">Light Spear, Swordsmen</td><td>12</td><td colspan="2" rowspan="2">4-6</td><td rowspan="2">0-12</td></tr>
<tr><td>Average</td><td>9</td></tr>
<tr><td colspan="2">Spearmen</td><td>Heavy Foot</td><td>Protected</td><td>Average</td><td>Undrilled</td><td>-</td><td>Defensive Spearmen</td><td>6</td><td>2/3 or all</td><td rowspan="2">8-12</td><td colspan="2">8-36</td></tr>
<tr><td colspan="2">Supporting archers</td><td>Light Foot</td><td>Unprotected</td><td>Average</td><td>Undrilled</td><td>Bow</td><td>-</td><td>5</td><td>1/3 or 0</td><td>0-18</td><td rowspan="3">6-28</td></tr>
<tr><td colspan="2" rowspan="2">Separately deployed archers</td><td>Light Foot</td><td>Unprotected</td><td>Average</td><td>Undrilled</td><td>Bow</td><td>-</td><td>5</td><td colspan="2">6-8</td><td rowspan="2">0-18</td></tr>
<tr><td>Medium Foot</td><td>Unprotected</td><td>Average</td><td>Undrilled</td><td>Bow</td><td>-</td><td>5</td><td colspan="2">6-8</td></tr>
</table>

SPECIAL FEATURES:

- Noble cavalry classified as Lancers, Swordsmen can be used at any date. They must be organized in battle groups of 4 or 6 bases. The army must include a minimum of 8 bases of them and cannot include more than 32. Noble cavalry classified as Light Spear, Swordsmen can only be used before 900 AD. They can be Superior or Average. All the bases in a battle group must be of the same quality, but different battle groups can be of different quality. The list specifies the different points costs. They must be organized in battle groups of 4 or 6 bases. The army cannot include more than 12 bases of them.
- The total number of bases of noble cavalry of all gradings cannot be more than 32. Before 900 AD the army can include both noble cavalry classified as Lancers, Swordsmen and noble cavalry classified as Light Spear, Swordsmen, but they cannot be in mixed battle groups.
- Spearmen battle groups can either be entirely of Heavy Foot Defensive Spearmen, or can have 2/3 of their bases as Heavy Foot Defensive Spearmen and 1/3 as Light Foot with Bow. If entirely of Heavy Foot they must be organized in battle groups of 8, 10 or 12 bases. If 2/3 Heavy Foot, 1/3 Light Foot, they must be organized in battle groups of 9 or 12 bases. The total number of bases of Heavy Foot Defensive Spearmen in the army must be at least 8 and not more than 36. The total number of bases of supporting archers in mixed battle groups

The Battle of Brunanburh, by Gerry Embleton. Taken from *Warrior* 3: Viking Hersir 793–1066 AD.

in the army cannot exceed 18.

- Separately deployed archers can either be Light Foot or Medium Foot. All the bases in a battle group must be of the same type, but different battle groups can be of different types. Separately deployed archers must be organized in battle groups of 6 or 8 bases. The total number of bases of separately deployed archers in the army cannot exceed 18.
- The total number of bases of supporting and separately deployed archers in the army must be at least 6 and cannot exceed 28.

APPENDIX 2 – THEMED TOURNAMENTS

A tournament based on the "Dark Age Europe" theme can include any of the armies listed in this book, but these cannot use any options only permitted after 1040 AD.

It can also include the following armies from our other army list books. These can only use options permitted between 496 AD and 1040 AD:

Field of Glory Companion 5: *Legions Triumphant: Imperial Rome at War*

Early Alan

Alamanni, Burgundi or Suebi from Early Frankish, Alamanni, Burgundi, Limigantes, Quadi, Rugii, Suebi or Turcilingi

Early Anglo-Saxon, Bavarian, Frisian, Old Saxon or Thuringian

Gepid or Early Lombard

Field of Glory Companion 7: *Decline and Fall: Byzantium at War*

Later Visigothic

Italian Ostrogothic

Lombard

Avar

Western Turkish (Khazar)

Early Bulgar

Pecheneg

INDEX

References to illustrations and maps are shown in **bold**